DRESS CODE

DRESS CODE

THE NAKED TRUTH ABOUT FASHION

MARI GRINDE ARNTZEN

REAKTION BOOKS

For Liam, Ivo and Bård – and my family,
who showed me how appearance and life can intertwine

Published by Reaktion Books Ltd
33 Great Sutton Street
London EC1V 0DX, UK
www.reaktionbooks.co.uk

This book was first published in Norwegian in 2013 by Forlaget Manifest AS
as *Kleskoden. Den nakne sannheten om mote*, by Mari Grinde Arntzen
Copyright © Forlaget Manifest 2013

First published in English 2015
English-language translation © Reaktion Books 2015
Translated by Kerri Pierce

This translation has been published with the financial assistance of NORLA

Printed and bound in Great Britain by Bell & Bain, Glasgow

A catalogue record for this book is available from the British Library

ISBN 978 1 78023 439 7

Contents

Introduction

I discovered a blue velvet ribbon in my mother's dressing table drawer. It was the mid '70s; I was maybe five years old and living in a small Norwegian industrial town. There were only a few clothes outlets – mostly for old women and men. I did not read newspapers or magazines, I watched children's TV for half an hour a day and the only advertisements I saw were some shampoo posters over at the local grocery. Nonetheless, I knew the ribbon was fashionable. I tied it tight around my throat like a piece of jewellery, since that was the style back then. This is my first memory of fashion – as something completely natural.

This book is the result of a reflection that struck me many years later. I had studied nature and the environment, development studies, social anthropology and journalism. Yet when I finally began work as a journalist, I began writing about fashion. First off, it was the beauty there that intrigued me, not to mention the challenge of predicting what was to come. And then the questions arose: Why do we spend so much time and money on dress? Why is it so important to have just the right look? Why does fashion change so quickly?

I wrote articles. I called researchers in Britain, Sweden, Denmark and the USA looking for answers. And I discovered an academic world that approached fashion in a way completely different from what I was used to in Norway. Fashion was not simply something vain and shallow. It was a method by which to study society, a tool one could use to understand people, as well as a visual form of communication. I wanted to write a book – on the language, power and identity project that fashion is. I wanted to undress fashion, article by article, as a phenomenon, a business and an art form. And yet beneath the layers I discovered something more. The truth is ugly as well.

In 1992, the UN's Earth Summit, held in Rio de Janeiro, issued a warning. Consumption by the wealthy countries was far too high; it would lead to global warming. With that would come extreme weather, natural catastrophes, famine and death. To avoid disaster, the wealthy nations had to reduce their consumption. As we know, consumption did not decrease. In Norway, where I live, it was the consumption of dress items – things meant to make ourselves and our environment more attractive – that increased the most.

We own twice as many clothes today as we did in 1980.[1] Cheap fashion hangs in everyone's closets. Apparently, poor quality and environmentally harmful production methods do nothing to lessen our appetite for a bargain. Nor do revelations of the use of child labour, miserable wages and inhuman working conditions.

Fashion has no sympathy. Our focus on personal gain and social survival seems to outweigh our common sense and concern for others. Even our future outlook recedes into the shadow of our desire to look great here and now.

We are dressing ourselves to death. And I wonder why.

The answer is found in fashion and in people. Yet what is it about fashion that blinds us so? What is it about people that makes being attractive more important than life itself?

I want to explore the history of the world's fifth-largest industry – worth trillions of dollars[2] – as well as the story behind one of the most pressing, and perhaps most unnecessary, problems confronting us today. The story of what fashion really is. Why the fashionable are powerful. And why beauty is so important to our lives.

By looking at fashion as an integral part of human existence, and the fashion industry as a kind of hacker in the brain, perhaps we can find answers that yield a more sustainable and better-dressed future.

ONE

Human Beings

What Fashion Actually Is

The thought struck them as they photographed some youths on Rotterdam's streets. The young people were dressed alike. In fact, they looked like carbon copies of each other. This phenomenon was nothing new to the two Dutch photographers. Teenagers are famous for imitating each other. Nonetheless, Ari Versluis and Ellie Uyttenbroek had an idea. Perhaps aping was common to everyone?

They began to study people in secret and found grandmothers in formless, colourless jackets with short, grey, coiffed hair. They found ordinary women in all-weather jackets with small bags on their backs. Long-haired girls in jeans, a top, a cardigan and with an oversize bag hanging from their forearm; hiphoppers in baggy tracksuits and caps positioned at identical angles; men in hoodies with shoulder bags slung across their chest; men in suits with no ties, but with bags hanging from their shoulders; 1940s-inspired babes with fitted pencil skirts and red lips . . .

Versluis and Uyttenbroek portrayed all these different, but ever-so-similar individuals. They grouped them according to style. Each group consisted of twelve portraits taken in the same medium. The venture became an art project, and then a full-time job, and was given the name 'Exactitudes', a combination of the two words at the project's heart: exact and attitudes. Since the mid-1990s, they have portrayed more than a hundred groups and held exhibitions throughout the world. 'Fifty years ago, your clothes said very little about who you were. Today clothes communicate a whole mass of things', Uyttenbroek explains. 'And if you look closely at what a person is wearing, there are a mass of details having to do with fashion, group belonging, subculture and how the dress code changes within different groups over time.'[1]

Out on the street people seem like a potpourri of different types and personalities. Yet when the two photographers separated individuals out and sorted them into groups, the hodgepodge gave way to clearly defined visual expressions with quite specific, indeed almost identical, attire. Humans and apes may have had a common ancestor in the distant past. But whereas apes are still plucking parasites from their fur out in the rainforest, humans shop for clothes at the mall, changing and washing their external coat day after day. Human beings live in highly developed societies, far removed from the primitive jungle. Nonetheless, we still have one thing in common with the apes: we are social creatures – we intercommunicate and live in groups. And, like apes, we mimic others of our kind. This fact influences fashion as a system.

In the *Austin Powers* movies, the villain, Dr Evil, clones a miniature copy of himself. This clone, who goes by the name of Mini-Me, dresses and acts just like his evil progenitor. However, when Mini-Me joins the good guys and becomes part of Team Powers in one of the films, he doesn't just change his affiliation, he also changes his wardrobe. He discards the Mao-esque madman's suit and dons Powers's signature ensemble – a striped and colourful suit with a 1960s-style cut. His bald little head now sprouts a wig identical to the hair of his new master. And although Mini-Me has never shown signs of impaired vision, he places a pair of Austin Powers glasses on top of his nose. Only then is he ready to work for British intelligence. In this way, Mini-Me emulates the group he wants to be a part of; he demonstrates his belonging through what he puts on. In the process, Mini-Me also reveals who he is.

The same story can be told in the opposite way. A person can show who he or she is by not emulating others. Documentary film-makers Albert and David Maysles wanted to make a movie about Lee Radziwill, the sister of Jackie Kennedy Onassis, and about her childhood in the fashionable Hamptons. One day towards the beginning of the 1970s, while the Maysles were visiting Radziwill, the telephone rang. Two of her relatives needed some help. The film-makers accompanied Radziwill to her relatives' house – a large, tumbledown affair in the middle of an overgrown yard that was known as Grey Gardens. It was here that Edith Bouvier Beale and her daughter, also Edith Bouvier Beale, lived. These two eccentric women, known as Big Edie and Little Edie, in the aristocratic Bouvier line had lived in isolation in that house for twenty years. There and then the Maysles dropped their project on Radziwill and started filming. Before the camera, the twosome paraded themselves for all they were worth. Some days it was like a cabaret. Little Edie sang and danced, while Big Edie hummed along. Other days were harrowing, full of despair over the hardships life had thrown their way. As a young woman, Little Edie had been a model in New York and Big Edie a singer and married to a respected lawyer. However, when Mr Beale left them in the 1930s, their financial security vanished.

Nonetheless, every day was a fashion show for Little Edie. She was like a child whenever she dressed up. She wrapped sweaters around her head, tied curtains around her body and wore her skirt upside down. Around there the norm was their manicured neighbours with their nice houses and jobs. They all resembled each other. Big and Little Edie, on the other hand, had cut the umbilical cord to life outside the fence. They did not emulate anyone – and no one wanted to emulate them. At least, not yet.

In 1975 the documentary *Grey Gardens* was released. The film gained attention because it showed that the famous and rich Kennedys had allowed Jackie's aunt and cousin to live in poverty. In narrow fashion and artistic circles it eventually became a cult film, but otherwise the Edies were forgotten. Twenty years passed. Then in 2006 Broadway swept the dust from the story and made a musical about the two women. Albert Maysles returned to the clipboard and the raw material from the first *Grey Gardens* became a second documentary in 2006.[2] In 2009 the feature film was released with Jessica Lange and Drew Barrymore in the roles of Big and Little Edie.[3]

However, the most interesting development of all emerged when the Italian fashion house Prada showed their 2007 spring collection. Suddenly, strolling across the catwalk were copies of Little Edie. The collection was inspired by her swimsuit dresses and the clothing she wore on her head. Little Edie, who had spent most of her life standing out, was suddenly in. Thirty years after the film and five years after her death, others were copying her. Edie's outlandish taste was now fashion. In this way, fashion revealed its underpinnings, showing what lay beneath the armour.

Fashion is propelled by two opposing human drives: the need to fit in and the need to stand out. On the one hand, society is composed of individuals, each with unique characteristics and personalities. However, these individuals are also woven together into a greater system – an organization where people live in groups that are more or less dependent on each other. And these two functions reflect themselves in two different human desires: we want to be individuals, be our own masters, our own fantastic masterworks. At the same time, we want to be part of a larger community. So we ape each other in order to fit in, and try to stand out in order to feel like ourselves. This tug-of-war occurs in every person every single day. Ideally, neither desire gets the upper hand. Too great a degree of difference or similarity can quickly tip over into something negative – as the American website *Huffington Post* reported during the 2009 MTV Video Music Awards: 'Oh no! Pink and Shakira showed up at the VMAS wearing the same Balmain studded leather dress!'[4] The event made headlines the world over. During the 2011 Cannes Film Festival, it happened again. Models Victoria Silvstedt and Bar Refaeli wore the same Roberto Cavalli dress. 'Fashion Catastrophe in Cannes', read the headline. 'Someone is going to get booted for this.'[5] It isn't acceptable to copy someone down to the smallest detail. It is embarrassing and, in the best case, ridiculous. If there is a conscious thought behind it, copying can even be regarded as malicious.

Indeed, sometimes too much similarity acts as a scare technique in movies. In *Single White Female*, the new tenant cuts her hair like her roommate and starts dressing in identical clothes.[6] We get the feeling that something is about to go horribly wrong. The new tenant is obviously not playing with a full deck. As it turns out later in the film, she is in fact an unstable killer.

But too much difference also comes at a price. Little Edie ultimately became a fashion icon. During the years of her life, however, she was considered strange and was left to herself. In 2007, a goth couple was attacked in a Lancashire park. The three teenagers who attacked them apparently didn't like the goth style. The boy survived but the girl died.[7]

Visually obvious faith-related attire like hijabs and niqabs also provoke reactions and have become significant political symbols in both a positive and negative sense – all according to where and by whom the garment is being worn.

For her part, the artist Lady Gaga sported a dress of raw meat at the MTV Video Music Awards in 2010. Despite this, she was not labelled a bizarre loner or an extreme provocateur. Popular culture is an exception. Blessed with a broader scope than other milieux, it ensures that an artist can actually benefit by appearing as a steak rather than a peacock. David Bowie, The Sex Pistols and Madonna have all reaped major benefits by standing out. The unusual and extreme are effective and acceptable forms of PR in the music industry.

In society, however, visual rules are more strongly connected to social norms. Individuality is a good thing, but it should only be taken so far. A person should demonstrate the ideal amount of belonging.

In practice, the two drives are like threads woven into one cloth. A single garment simultaneously holds a plethora of symbols and meanings. The design historian Joanne Turney has among other things conducted research into knitwear and, in particular, why it is regarded as safe, protective and cosy. Strangely, however, a hooded jacket changed the situation completely, inspiring sudden fear.

In 2005, the Bluewater shopping centre in Kent banned their customers from wearing hoodies. Of course, hooded sweatshirts and jackets remained for sale in the shops. It was not the hood itself that was the problem. The ban was a measure to stop to what they termed 'anti-social behaviour' – that is to say, to stop young, possible criminals from disturbing the shopping idyll by using swear words and inappropriate conduct. What these youths had in common was that they often wore hoods. The ban prompted a large debate across Britain. Is it really acceptable to eliminate a social problem by removing a clothing item? Is gang-related crime not a problem requiring a social solution? Turney began to draw together the strands of her argument.

Historically, hoodies are a recognized part of African American street culture. At the same time, hooded jackets also have a cultural history in which evil and threatening figures are often represented wearing hoods. Death wears a long hooded cape. The evil emperor Palpatine in the *Star Wars* films uses one as well. The decaying, ghost-like dementors in *Harry*

Potter all wear hoods, as do members of the Ku Klux Klan. Turney also examined the human factors associated with the hood. It hides the wearer's identity and makes them unrecognizable and effectively nearly inhuman. Yet hoodies are not only a garment of evil. They are well suited to a certain phase in a young person's life. Just as the jacket defines them as being outside dull, 'square' society, it also designates them as part of a narrower fellowship – a group. It gives them a feeling of belonging. The garment's hood and shape enables them to hide an identity they haven't yet discovered. It can protect the vulnerable young person inside. In this way, something as simple as a hood can be regarded as purveying significant ideas, as a tool in a personal, as well as political, project.[8]

Fundamental to dress codes is the need to fit in. However, even when playing the mirror game of aping others, one still has a little voice whispering in the ear – you are not like all the rest, you want to be different and unique. And like a little devil on one shoulder and an angel on the other, the two desires begin to negotiate with each other. Turney thinks this negotiation technique is something with which everyone is familiar. 'Everyone knows how to dress. That is something we have in us from our earliest childhood', she says.[9] Children quickly understand isolated facts such as which clothes go with hot or cold weather. After a certain age, children also learn that it isn't acceptable to run around the streets naked. As teenagers and adults, they become acquainted with even more visual rules, such as the fact that brides wear white to their weddings and a pink catsuit has no place at a funeral. Additionally, there are cultural variations established by your background, where you live and how you want to be perceived as the person you are. People in New York will probably dress differently to those in Anchorage, Alaska – and not just because of the distance between the two cities or the variations in climate. Even in Britain, towns and cities only a couple of hours apart have different dress codes. Indeed, within London there are various fit-in-and-stand-out codes. A person living in the trendy district of Shoreditch in the east of the city will dress differently to someone living in affluent Kensington in the west. And as a person passes in and out of these zones, they alter between fitting in and sticking out – entirely according to their address, attire and situation.

Yet Turney also believes that the way a person feels within their environment influences what they choose to wear. If a person is surrounded by rail-thin people, there is a chance they will feel overweight, even if they are not. Because of external factors affecting their feelings, the person will choose clothes that compensate for the imagined fatness, selecting garments that boost self-confidence or that hide the body. On top of all this comes fashion.

According to Turney, 'Fashion's nature is new and variable, and very few are actually wearing what is truly fashionable. After all, not many people have the means to change their wardrobe as often as fashion changes. Nonetheless, people are aware of fashion and demonstrate their understanding through the styles, colours and textiles they put on.'[10] We acquire this understanding through the access we have to information from TV, magazines, newspapers, advertisements and the Internet, as well as what we see out on the street and in the shops. The image of what is fashionable is, so to speak, open and accessible to all. Learning, comparing, updating, assessing and negotiating – these are things we do all the time and extremely quickly. We absorb huge quantities of information every day, reading the images and understanding them. Therefore, Turney believes, everyone knows what fashion is, even if they claim not to. Namely, one must understand fashion in order to reject it.

Why do people transform a functional action – that of dressing ourselves – into a complicated social and mental exercise? Turney believes it all comes down to competition. In every society there is a degree of struggle between belonging to the group and demonstrating one's individuality. And since the late 1940s and early '50s, society has increasingly tended to have an individualized focus. Human beings may act like sheep, but on an individual level they also want to be seen as unique. And if this motivation isn't quite as pressing as the will to survive, it still boils down to the desire to position oneself within the group – to come across as attractive. Dress is a form of Darwinism.

The need to fit in and the need to stand out are like the positive and negative electrodes in a starter battery. When it comes to dress and adornment, the reaction between them is what jump-starts the machine. However, in order to ensure that the machine actually runs, something more is required. The motor needs regular refuelling in order to generate forward movement – something that guarantees people never forget to negotiate between the need to be oneself and the need to be part of a community. The motor requires fuel – and that fuel is fashion.

What goes into the fuel cannot be determined by a single recipe. Fashion's only certain component is its variability.

Why Fashion Changes

'There will be rabbits', proclaimed Li Edelkoort. It was during a trend seminar at Copenhagen's Bella Center in 2006 that the Dutch trend forecaster predicted that rabbits would be the next big thing. From the room came a question – how did she actually know it would be a rabbit and not a hamster or some other rodent? 'I can feel it', Edelkoort answered firmly.[11]

Like a meteorologist who predicts the rain before a cloud appears in the sky, Li Edelkoort can sniff out trends several years in advance. She herself claims that in 1972 she already foresaw the period we are just now entering:

Naturally, ideas about the future don't just materialize out of thin air. They are already present, even if they aren't so easily recognizable. In order to be able to say something about what will influence people's actions, or what priorities they will have in, for example, two years, five years, or ten years, you have to have the ability to understand what is stirring in society in general. I have a strong instinct for understanding what people are feeling and thinking; it is constantly operating – even now. The more space I give it, the more I rely on it, the more developed it becomes.[12]

This hypersensitivity has proved a goldmine; the audience is willing to shell out hundreds of dollars just to hear the prophetess speak. Knowing the future is worth the price. There is always something new ahead – and Edelkoort hit the target dead on: she was right about the rabbits.

Maria Mackinney-Valentin, who researches fashion trends, heard the rabbit exchange. It made her think. How can a person actually predict trends when they are so brief and irrational? In that case, is there not some less precarious and more exact method by which they might be analysed? Earlier Mackinney-Valentin had worked as a journalist for various fashion magazines and had always scratched her head over statements like 'Now black is in' and 'New this season: red lipstick'. How can red lipstick be considered new? Cleopatra was using it before Jesus was born. Indeed, a magazine might claim that English landed gentry, '20s bohemian, '60s sex kitten, rock chic à la '70s and white trash Americana are all in at once. The trend researcher wanted to tidy things up.

Her determination became a doctoral thesis mapping out the dominant theories as to why and how trends change.[13] These theories explain fashion's mutability. 'We have the feeling it is a sense, but that sense is rooted in other factors',

Mackinney-Valentin explains. 'One may be that we follow the herd. At the same time, we have the paradoxical desire to appear as individuals and distinguish ourselves from the group. As a result, the sense that something in particular will be the next thing to come is a sense that you are going to alter your appearance. You have looked one way long enough and now it is time for a change.'[14]

Once again the pendulum swings between the individual and the group, between fitting in and standing out. However, the pendulum also swings to a variety of outer points. Black and white, narrow and wide, jagged and straight. If something has been in style for a period of time, it will be counterbalanced by something suggestive of the opposite. After fitted jeans come baggy jeans. After a low waist a high one. This is one of fashion's most obvious movements. Yet fashion is more than just an oscillating weight. People also respond to the things happening around them – and this creates new fashion.

Tool 1: The Zeitgeist – The Watch in the Tool Chest

When the new century was approaching, fashion stripped down. It became simpler, colourless, rather futuristic, but most of all it held its breath. The suspense surrounding what would happen when the calendar showed 1 January 2000 materialized in a millennial look. Just as the plastic bodies of mannequins are wrapped in brown paper when there is a sale, so fashionable clothes in 1999 were reduced to the bare essentials. They were a blank sheet upon which the future might write. The collective mood – or zeitgeist – materialized in the fashion scene.

Isolated events can have the same effect. In Autumn 2005, what began with two dead teenagers in France would influence the fashion house Dior's collection. Bouna, fifteen, and Zyed, seventeen, both from the poor Paris suburb of Clichy-sous-Bois, feared the police were pursuing them and so hid in an electricity substation. The previous week, then interior minister Nicolas Sarkozy had announced that he would clean up and mercilessly wage war against crime in the Paris suburbs. Both boys died of electric shock. The tragedy in Clichy-sous-Bois acted like petrol thrown on a fire. Riots began in the suburb where the boys died, but quickly spread to other parts of France.[15] While young people set fire to cars, schools and police stations, John Galliano travelled to the south of France to find inspiration for his newest collection. The insurrection made a strong impression on Dior's former head designer and he hightailed it back to the fashion house's corset factory.

The Spring/Summer collection of 2006 would be created in the spirit of the revolt. He wanted to convey the nerve of what shook France there and then. So Galliano swept the dust from the straitjacket – the corset – and chose the colours red, black and white, complete with blood-like flecks along the skirt hem. Upon the models' necks was written '1789' – the year of the French Revolution.[16]

As Mackinney-Valentin observes: 'Trends are not just a part of the fashion industry. They are a way to communicate who you are and who you want to be. They are a way to address the things that make us uncomfortable in society. They are a way to exchange meanings and political theories.'[17]

Tool 2: The Social Theory – The Glue in the Tool Chest

The concept of someone wanting to stand out from the masses, and the masses in turn copying them, is perhaps the most employed theory of all. 'Traditionally, it was a matter of wanting to climb the social ladder and appear like the social class above you. However, now it is all different', Mackinney-Valentin explains.[18] When actress Katie Holmes appeared in an oversized, checked lumberjack shirt and old jeans, women the world over copied her. She was a fashion icon and a woman walking around in shapeless work clothes meant for men. She stood out and inspired others to imitate her. The trend trickled down the system, from the fashion gurus at the top of the hierarchy to the fashion followers below. By emulating Holmes they were trying to ascend to her level. But we can also interpret Holmes's shirt choice as an upward movement in the fashion system as a whole. She elevated a working-class garment up to her fashionable sphere.

At the same time, the social theory also concerns horizontal movements. In different social environments in the same city, for example, a lumberjack shirt can have varying status. In some environments it might be a shirt used by older, working-class men and have an across the board low status. In other arenas it can be a symbol of something young and hip.

Tool 3: The Seduction Theory – Viagra in the Tool Chest

One of the longest-standing theories concerns the sexually seductive power of clothes. Until relatively recently in the West, women were economically dependent on men. In order to secure her future, a woman had to hold a man's interest. She did this, among other things, with clothing. Through shifting focus to the body, and by hiding some parts and revealing others, she kept the man's attention. These changes preserved his interest and sustained trends.[19]

Today the seduction theory is relevant in a different way. The checked lumberjack shirt isn't a sheer and revealing thing that shows a woman's breasts, bottom and thighs. It is big, thick and masculine. Nonetheless, it can be seen as a seductive trend. Only an extremely feminine woman or one who is comfortable with her own sexuality feels at ease in such an outfit. Even though the shirt covers those areas of the female body traditionally perceived as arousing, the garment says something about the wearer's inherently feminine and sexual qualities. Seduction happens here on an ideological plane.

Tool 4: The Business Theory – The Wallet in the Tool Chest

Money drives wardrobe changes. Every season has a new look because the fashion industry wants to make a profit. A swinging pendulum perpetually generates the demand to snap up whatever is new – at least, if the industry is clever enough to devise some trend not seen before, or some novel detail that reinvents an existing item. Therefore, every season has a specific item that the major fashion magazines declare to be that autumn or spring's winning look. Whether it is a camel-coloured coat or a pair of gladiator sandals – as soon as that season's victors are announced, they are seen in stores and on the high street. In autumn 2009, the Balmain jacket was declared the next big thing. The financial crisis had seized the globe and fashion consisted of several classic and timeless pieces – like the black suit jacket. However, while most producers focused on the plain cut, the fashion house Balmain did something a little different with their jacket. They created their very own Balmain shoulders – a sculpted and pointy variety that made shoulders seem narrower and higher. The jacket was a hit. The year passed and another autumn came around. Now pointy shoulders no longer had the same edge – it was time to find a new winner. This time the champion was Burberry Prorsum's aviator jacket. A big, leather, sheepskin-lined pilot jacket – miles from the previous year's fitted, sharply tailored item.

Of course, another move is to switch colours. Classics such as the trench coat can survive for years, but proclaiming beige to be that year's colour when most people have only black is to create demand for the new one. It is like waves washing onto the beach, always bringing something new with them, whether it is water from further out, a dead starfish or a plank they picked up along the way. The eternal circulation of water and debris is endless. This movement is what drives the sea. So it goes with fashion as well.

Tool 5: Neomania – The One-armed Bandit in the Tool Chest

This theory holds that whatever is new becomes trendy simply because it is new. It is postmodernism's attribute. By combining the old with the new and the expensive with the cheap, we show that trends mean nothing to us. We toy with the limitless, and when we grow bored, we create some new combination.[20] As the philosopher Lars Svendsen puts it, 'Fashion is irrational in the sense that it seeks for change for the sake of change.'[21]

With that, Maria Mackinney-Valentin had readied the tool chest for use. However, there was still a small screw missing, one that would hold the whole thing together. The five main theories explained the causes behind wardrobe changes. But fashion isn't simply one long chain of new creations that pop up. Fashion also concerns repetition.

During the first years of the twenty-first century, plenty of old styles were regurgitated. It seemed that fashion was caught in an eternal cycle of old trends that never completely left. The 1980s, the '20s, the '60s and the '40s . . . the styles appeared again and again – often simultaneously. Maria's tool chest explained the connection between human life and visual expression, and that the connection was driven by a dichotomous force. Yet it gave no clear picture of the way retro fashion actually functions. It lacked a model that could describe the conditions for trend growth. So Mackinney-Valentin dug deeper – literally speaking: she discovered an organic model physically located below ground.

In 1980 the French philosophers Gilles Deleuze and Félix Guattari published *A Thousand Plateaus*, a book that made use of a botanical root system as a model for something more: they believed the rhizome – a type of plant stem that spreads below ground to form new roots and shoots – could conceptualize the world in which we live. Tuber by tuber, rhizomes – such as the ginger root – grow underground with no specific core. In contrast to the tree, which has a trunk attached to roots beneath the surface, the rhizome perpetually moves in new directions, formations and relations. Here and there the rhizome sends up new shoots, while other shoots die off. All the while, the rhizome persists down there in the dark. It is an organic network constantly undergoing self-development and never actually expiring. The philosophers used this root system as an explanatory model in their work. The same could apply to fashion. The rhizome could illustrate fashion's inner life.[22]

Take Dita Von Teese, for example. Through her, the 1940s movie-star look acquired a new spring. The burlesque dancer and style icon looks like a sensual Hollywood wartime chanteuse – a dark copy of Rita Hayworth. However, Dita Von Teese also infuses something punky into the old elegance. Mackinney-Valentin, inspired by the theory of the rhizome, has developed a theory of the ginger root as it relates to fashion; according to her, Dita is not a direct copy of Rita. Instead, she is a tuber who has grown out of an entirely different place on the rhizome. She is a distinct variation from a different time period, not a copycat or a clone of the glamorous 1940s woman.

'You can regard fashion as a whole series of ginger tubers that continue to develop, form new constellations and interact with each other', Mackinney-Valentin explains. 'In Dita Von Teese we have some sort of punk Rita Hayworth with roots reaching back to the '40s and '70s. In this way, the tubers converse and exchange.'[23]

Dita Von Teese grew up in a working-class family in a small Michigan town. She inherited her interest in old Hollywood movies from her mother. Where the fascination for glamorous undergarments comes from no one really knows. When she was a teenager and the time came to get her first bra, her disappointment over the white cotton thing her mother bought her was apparently so severe that Dita travelled by herself to a lingerie shop that carried a black and lace model. According to Dita herself, when she came out of that store she was one blissful and old-fashioned lady. This 'unmodern' trait, as Von Teese has termed it, is something she made a point of later. Yet when she was asked if she would have been happier living at some other time, her answer was neither yes nor no. Instead, she answered that the question itself told her she was living right at the time she should. The question told her that people needed her in the here and now.[24]

Von Teese has it right: fashion needs people like her. Von Teese was unconventional and old-fashioned when she began dressing like the old pin-up model Bettie Page. A teenager in a small American town just did not do that in the 1980s. Both Von Teese and Little Edie of Grey Gardens stood out so much that they simply could not fit in. However, with time they inspired the fashion industry and ended up becoming style icons themselves. Both are rare flowers that have seeded and multiplied. What was at first quirky was later assimilated by the majority. Fashion has to change in order to be fashion, and for that to happen some individuals must stick out a little and bring something different, something new, something visual for the rest to imitate. But before a new thing becomes fashionable, it must be widely adopted.

The concept of what is new must acquire a greater degree of fitting in than standing out. The weight that balances the two desires must end up at a particular fashion point. If the weight swings too far in the direction of standing out, the result is no longer fashion. The same applies if it tends too much towards fitting in. There is a sweet spot right in the middle. Achieving this balance is a dynamic process; it will never pause or cease, for fashion follows the same pattern as people themselves:

there is an eternal negotiation between being an individual and being part of a group. Fashion is driven by the mental line dance we perform every day. As a result, it fits into people's lives like a hand into a glove. It weaves itself into what people have already done. The motor is fully assembled; fashion oils it and provides the fuel that enables the machine to drive further and perhaps faster than it otherwise would. In this way, fashion has assumed a central place in society and in human life. It creeps beneath a person's skin, gets inside their head and becomes part of what is perhaps the most personal thing of all: an individual's self-image and identity.

Why Dressing is Me

Michael Jackson once told Oprah Winfrey in an interview that he did not like to see himself in the mirror. He would much rather avoid his own reflection. Oprah widened her eyes in a sympathetic, almost tearful expression. One moment Jackson was talking about his tough childhood and difficult relationship with his father; the next about why he avoided mirrors. This interview was held after Michael Jackson was accused of molesting a thirteen-year-old boy; Jackson needed to re-establish a more human image of himself and to increase public sympathy. He succeeded. Admitting that you don't like to look at yourself in the mirror is interpreted as meaning you don't like yourself as a person.

Apparel and other forms of dress serve a double function. They protect you from the elements and the eyes of others, but they also reveal something about the individual. The body becomes a channel of communication that discloses who you are.

The mirror image as *something more* is also a theme found in fairy tales. In 'Snow White and the Seven Dwarfs', the evil queen's mirror has the magical properties of a high judge, one who can determine the fairest in the land. The mirror chooses Snow White – the beauty whose heart is also noble. The choice appears to be just. The queen/witch may have a beautiful face, but she is evil and bad-tempered and cannot, therefore, truly be attractive. For it is only when the mirror relates to both the inner and outer qualities of a person that the choice feels right.

In Hans Christian Andersen's 'The Ugly Duckling', the duckling interprets his reflection incorrectly when he spies himself in the water. He considers his exterior only in relation to others, and completely forgets to see the enormous potential he has within – namely, that he is in fact a swan. So he comes to the wrong conclusion – that he is ugly.

In *Harry Potter and the Philosopher's Stone*, Harry does the opposite. He ignores the physical facts when he looks into the magical Mirror of Erised. All the mirror shows is Harry's greatest dream – to be reunited with his dead parents. That is not a good thing either. The outer dimension is entirely forgotten. Harry sits spellbound in front of the mirror until Professor Dumbledore tells him that the mirror only leads to misery and insanity. The best thing he can do is live his life as it actually is.

Yet the mirror is a straightforward aid that enables us to see whether certain colours go together and whether our hair is sticking out in all directions. At the same time, the mirror conceptualizes invisible dimensions such as thoughts, beliefs, feelings, dreams and mental states. It reflects both outer and inner worlds, as well as the interplay between the two. People thus regard the exterior as a materialization of identity.

In modern culture, people no longer look so much inside themselves to find their identity – but are just as apt to look without.[25] The mirror has become more important to us. The construction of personal identity has become a body project. As Lars Svendsen puts it: 'We seek identity in the body, and clothes are an immediate continuation of the body. That is also why clothes are so important to us: they are closest to our body.'[26]

In the film *Terminator 2: Judgment Day*, for example, the cyborg known as the Terminator, played by Arnold Schwarzenegger, is naked when he is sent to the present day from the future. His mission is to help a teenager who will eventually become a rebel and save humankind from the machine's autocracy. In the dead of night the humanoid robot makes his way to a bar. He needs to find clothing. The Terminator's body is bursting with muscles and, with a rather staccato-like motion, he approaches the drinkers. His face is expressionless and his eyes empty and hard. But the Terminator is naked, and when he walks in, the people around him stop and study him with intense and naive curiosity. Some smile, others sneer impudently, but no one is afraid. They have no idea how to respond to the naked man. They do not equate his muscles and steely gaze with something threatening. Instead, they react with astonishment and ridicule. Even when he pauses before a long-haired man in a black leather jacket and trousers at the pool table and says, 'I need your clothes, your boots and your motorcycle' – nobody shows any concern. They just laugh. It is only when the Terminator responds by throwing a couple of guys through the window and stabbing another through the shoulder that they realize he is dangerous. At this point they become terrified and scurry away.

The naked cyborg isn't seen for what it actually is. It is not until he dons black leather and sets himself astride a huge motorcycle wearing dark sunglasses and then drives into the night that he signals his true self. The clothing reveals his identity. He is a tough guy, a killing machine with no remorse, whom most people would do well to fear.

The Norwegian fashion journal *Personae* explains the difference between the naked and the clothed body. 'Arraying oneself in textiles and jewellery . . . is inextricably tied to cultural development, to identity and to individuality. Other than as a form of representation, the naked body has no place in culture. Nakedness disindividualizes and dehumanizes.'[27]

The same interpretation can be found outside academic circles. The Hollywood stylist and designer Rachel Zoe, who is best known for exclaiming 'Oh my God!' and 'Awesome!' when shopping for vintage haute couture in the reality documentary series *The Rachel Zoe Project*, has remarked that style should communicate who you are without saying a word. In fact, Zoe became world famous for dressing celebrities in styles identical to her own – something that earned the celebrities the nickname 'Zoebots'. Nonetheless, the American shopping queen does touch upon something central here: there is an expectation out there that the visual dimension should summarize one's identity.

A typical first encounter with the Italian fashion journalist Anna Piaggi was like being blinded; like moving from a pitch-black room out into the sharp sun. Then – slowly – your eyes grew accustomed to the light and, bit by bit, you began to see again. Even at 80-plus years, Anna Piaggi dyed her hair blue, painted blue eyeshadow around her eyes panda-fashion, coloured her face white and painted her lips red, with a sharp 'v' on her upper lip. On each cheek she wore a round red spot, like a clown. She was the woman behind the distinctive *doppie pagine* ('double pages') spreads in Italian *Vogue*, and was famous in the fashion world for her precise trendspotting and her creative whims. Piaggi's circle of friends – including Chanel designer Karl Lagerfeld, milliner Stephen Jones and shoe designer Manolo Blahnik – ensured she received haute couture right on her doorstep, virtually still warm from the catwalk.

Unsurprisingly, though, Piaggi was most famous for how she looked. As well as the exclusive clothes and bizarre make-up, she went around in small, odd and completely non-functional hats, not to mention carrying a cane too tiny to offer any support. She was a mixture of punk, clown and Marie Antoinette.

So if this reflected Piaggi's inner persona – who was she? Manolo Blahnik believes that appearance for Piaggi was communication.[28] She wanted to entertain the people she met with what she was wearing, and she took her cue from whom she was meeting and in what context. Out of this, Piaggi shaped herself. If it was a particularly special occasion, she would call up Stephen Jones for a new custom-made hat. When she was due to be photographed by the British newspaper *The Observer*, she showed up in a hat with a picture of Prince William on it – a sly reference to journalism and the press. At other times the coupling was somewhat more diffuse. When Karl Lagerfeld held a ball, and the evening's theme was Venice, most people showed up dressed as Venetian dukes and duchesses. But not Anna. She came dressed as a fisherwoman and arrived with a basket full of seaweed and crabs on her head. Around her neck she had slung a pair of dead pigeons she had bought at the butcher's. When it was nearly midnight the pigeons began to bleed. Piaggi was forced to go home – just like Cinderella.[29]

Anna Piaggi was not herself when she was naked and unmade. At that point, her bedroom door was closed and no one was allowed to see who she was. Anna Piaggi was only Anna Piaggi when she had dressed for the people she was going to meet. Together with the pigments, perfumes and parabens, her identity was found in make-up, not in a natural state. It emerged in the cultivated version of herself – and in the meeting between that self and others. That made Anna Piaggi normal.

What Happens When I Get Dressed

What happens when we choose the clothes that we do? Does fashion steer the process? British fashion researcher Sophie Woodward wanted to discover just that. The question sent her into the bedrooms of 27 ordinary British women for nearly a year and a half. For Sadie, one of Woodward's subjects, finding an outfit is a battle. It is evening and Sadie is wearing pyjamas. Before going to bed she has to decide what to wear the next day. After work she will be going straight to a farewell party with some friends. First she picks out her shoes: a pair of high heels, the heels of which are, of all things, shiny, pink and metallic. Sadie parades them in front of the mirror and inspects them from different angles. She has never been able to find an outfit that goes with them. The clothes have to match, yet not distract from the shoes. She hits on a cream-coloured miniskirt. That works. Now for the top. Still nothing fits with metallic pink shoes and a cream-coloured skirt. Sadie is at a loss. New clothes are not an option; she doesn't have the funds. Suddenly, inspiration strikes. She sees herself full length in the mirror and realizes that the light pink top she already has on – her pyjama top – is a perfect fit. Can she wear PJs out in the city? Yes. Sadie decides it will do.[30]

Woodward believes that Sadie is a good example of the basic process at work when we get dressed. So, when Sadie is again going out, Woodward returns to her apartment with pen and paper. This time she is meeting Warren – a date. The cream-coloured skirt and pink top from last time did the trick, so she settles on them a second time. Warren was not at the last party, and so hasn't seen her in the outfit yet. Still, she drops the pink metallic heels and goes for a pair of pink flipflops instead. It all has to be suitably casual, suitably sexy, suitably feminine – suitably *her*. Sadie has showered, smeared tanning lotion on her legs since this year she could not afford a holiday, and is blow-drying her hair. A whole twenty minutes is spent just on drying. At the end, she sits down to put on deodorant. Her hair can wait; now she wants to try on clothes. In front of the mirror she twists and turns to get just the right reflection. Does my G-string show under my skirt? Sadie approaches Woodward, who is sitting on the floor. 'Can you see my arse?', she asks, bending over. The entire clothing process takes three hours. This is a girl who would rather be late for work than drop her daily ritual. She has applied make-up, plucked her eyebrows, ironed her hair because her straightener is broken, sprinkled herself with body glitter, put on clothes and jewellery, and sprayed a perfume squirt into the air and walked through it.[31] By the time Sadie is dressed, nothing has been overlooked. And no movement has gone unnoticed by Woodward by the time Sadie flies out the door.

All the women who participated in the fieldwork prioritized time and energy for dressing. Sadie's three-hour ritual was one of the longest battles, but all the women considered and negotiated with themselves as they stood in front of the mirror. Did they look a bit fat in this dress? Did these two colours really go together? Was this skirt really 'them'? Even though the questions concerned what was on the surface, they still found the answers within. As Woodward explains:

> The act of getting dressed takes place at least once a day and as such is ubiquitous and experienced by all women irrespective of age, occupation, sexuality, religion, ethnicity or interest in clothing. It is the occasion when women have to negotiate their bodies, respectability, style, status, and their self-perception and is therefore a crucial moment in understanding why women choose to wear what they wear.[32]

The act of dressing is almost described like a daily Big Bang in the individual's life. In one fell swoop the body's outer shell is observed and compared and adjusted to what one finds within. There and then the surface is modelled according to one's self-conception. Accordingly, the answer to why the individual wears what she does lies not just in fashion. The outer packaging is also a result of the meeting with the self and the conclusion one draws from it. When Sadie stands in the pink pyjama top glancing into her wardrobe, for example, it isn't just clothes she sees but also an arsenal of possibilities and limitations regarding the person she feels she is and the one whom she wishes to be. The clothes are like pieces in a puzzle she assembles to show a picture of what she thinks is herself. This picture also varies with the social context into which she is entering. She doesn't grab the telephone like Anna Piaggi to order a new hat from Stephen Jones. But she does the same thing when she creates a suitable new self by rethinking the clothes and shoes that she already has. And during the seconds or minutes she spends looking at her own reflection, she also encounters the self she wants to be and to appear to be. The act of dressing is self-construction. When the individual is building a self-identity, it isn't enough to sketch an inner drawing of oneself and to erect a mental structure no one else can see. Identity is also something that must be made apparent. The body's outer packaging is, therefore, a part of the total self-conception. And as you stand there confronted with your own reflection, studying everything from pimples to wrinkles only to zoom out full body to check whether these colours actually match – you simultaneously ask: Is that me?

In the film *The Matrix*, reality has several levels. Machines have taken over the world; human beings have been downgraded to battery status. Without knowing it, their bodies are imprisoned in liquid-filled cocoons. Their bodily energy is being transformed into the power source keeping the machines running, while their consciousness tells them they are leading completely normal lives. The machines manipulate the human mind into believing that everything is just like it was before the machines took over. They go to work, they eat, they love and party and despair. Such is the Matrix: a computer program that implants a virtual life into human heads as they lie there and discharge. However, the main character, the desk worker and computer hacker Thomas Anderson, is freed by a resistance group. They think that he is the one person who can liberate humanity from the machine's brutal regime. He is The One – he is Neo.

For his part, Anderson does not believe this is true at the beginning of the first movie. He can't see for himself that he is capable and courageous enough to save humanity. After all, he is no Jesus Christ; instead he is a rather incongruous underdog who feels that something isn't right, but doesn't know exactly what or why. The rebels begin to train Anderson. By entering and exiting the Matrix, they can manipulate and carry out the struggle against the machines. When those who have been liberated enter the fictitious virtual world, they appear as they perceive themselves to be. The person they think they are is projected through clothes and accessories. In the beginning, Anderson is a rather sorry sight. His hair is lifeless and his clothes are middle of the road sweaters and trousers. However, as he takes up the fight against the machines and realizes that his abilities are far from average, his style changes bit by bit. Like the others in the resistance, he becomes darker and tougher. He acquires sunglasses. Even his hair has a bit more oomph to it. Slowly but surely, Anderson becomes convinced that he really is Neo. In the end, dressed in a long black coat, he looks like a leader and a saviour. He is cool and he is invincible. He is and truly appears to be the chosen one.

This is an open line of communication between an individual's inner and outer layers. But the line doesn't simply end with a back-and-forth relay between the surface and the core. It is also connected to a larger network. For it isn't just one's self-conception that is expressed here. Human beings are social creatures who also visually communicate with their surroundings. Clothes place us socially in society – and we know it. We know others see and judge us by our appearance. So we apply several different gazes when we look in the mirror. These gazes are akin to surveillance cameras mounted in a variety of rooms. Flush with the ceiling, they hang without the individual noticing the lenses following their movements. And all the images from the different cameras are linked to a common network that ends in a control room.

Within this room, furthermore, there is a control panel where all the images are displayed side by side on different screens. Taken together, the screens yield a complete picture. However, the watchman whose job it is to follow the action can jump from screen to screen and can zoom in on whatever he might find interesting. This watchman is the individual herself and the cameras are the different gazes a person applies.

One surveillance camera is mounted in the room where self-image and identity are located. This room is under constant renovation. Everything an individual experiences and feels is gathered together here and the camera follows the construction process. The camera documents who I think I am.

A second surveillance camera hangs in another room and keeps track of the individual's physical appearance. These images are continuously being compared with the images taken from the self-identity room. Together the two cameras check to make sure that the individual's physical appearance corresponds with the person's idea of who she is. For the individual has an ideal version of herself and it is this sense or concept that is translated into physical appearance. It is here that the ideal encounters hard reality. After all, a person's physical appearance doesn't always correspond with the ideas she has about herself. Then again, there are also more surveillance cameras on the lookout.

The third camera hangs in the room where the individual encounters others. It follows the way she visually fits in with the crowd. This helps her to project herself beforehand into the social contexts she will enter, providing a picture of how these encounters will look. 'It is the I that perceives the me', as Woodward puts it.[33]

The final surveillance camera is cleverly placed. It has been snuck into other people's heads and follows what others will likely think when they see her. All these devices also study the individual while she dresses – unconsciously and automatically, so to speak. When she can't make the images correspond, she suddenly has nothing to wear. Crisis time. If, on the other hand, she likes what she sees, she has succeeded in achieving harmony between the 'I' and the 'me'. In this case, physical appearance nicely agrees with the ideal image she has of herself. Is this true for both men and women? Yes, but some differences do seem to exist. The final surveillance camera, the one installed in other people's heads, is employed more by women than men. Women seem to place greater emphasis on what that camera tells them, and are more concerned with seeing themselves through the eyes of others.

An experiment involving swimsuits gave clear evidence that this was the case. One after the other, women and men were placed alone in a room with a mirror and asked to solve mathematical equations. Their mathematical skills were all essentially the same. However, they were also asked to solve the problems in swimwear. That was no big deal for the men. Clad in swim trunks, they calculated away. In contrast, the women had more problems concentrating. The reflection of themselves in swimwear distracted them from their given task. They were tempted to look at themselves from the outside. The conclusion was: women are more concerned with seeing their bodies through the eyes of others.[34]

The usual perception is that the ideal image of body and appearance is media-generated. The overwhelming impetus is to look like the models in the advertisements and fashion magazines, and to walk around dressed like red-carpet celebrities. Woodward, however, believes that the ideal image is more complex than that. The ideal or picture of the ultimate 'I' is also influenced by personal factors like one's childhood and life experiences. God only knows what Anna Piaggi experienced, but in Sadie's case Woodward believes that the visible version can be traced back to, among other things, a basically attractive appearance and various jobs where Sadie has been admired for just that. Other's gazes and observations have supplied her with feedback on what works and what doesn't, and this feedback has become part of the overall mixture of who she is. When Sadie, for example, was bitten by the exercise bug, she underwent the painful experience of losing herself in gym clothes. Her project was to turn out an even better and healthier version of herself. Sadie began working out almost every day after work, but the combination of ample make-up and exercise proved to be a difficult one. When Sadie sweated, her make-up ran, so she decided to go to work wearing less make-up. That got a reaction. Her colleagues pulled her aside and asked if everything was okay. She did not look like her usual self. After a while, all these comments made Sadie herself feel like something was not right. She looked at herself in the mirror and realized she did not recognize the person she saw. She had to return to her daily make-up ritual. Sadie's true self was a made-up one. The natural version was unnatural. The cultivated image was Sadie's true 'I'.[35]

TWO

The Democracy

How Fashion and the Individual Intersect

'Girls are insane', says Jörgen Appelqvist.[1]

On an early spring day in 2007, the CEO of the Swedish bargain fashion chain Gina Tricot surveys his lifework. Five minutes ago he opened a new 1,000-square-metre store in a new city and a new country. Now that store is crawling with young women – shopping-crazed women. Appelqvist shakes his head. The girls load their arms with garment after garment. The line to the dressing room is 10 metres long, and while dozens patiently wait for an opening, others stand in the middle of the floor trying on clothes over the ones they have on.

'We men aren't smart consumers', Appelqvist says. 'We shop three, four times a year and buy three sets of pants, four shirts and four ties. If we approach our girls and ask what they want, at first they don't answer. So you put the words into their mouths: Do you frequently want what's new? Yes. And low prices? Yes. And to have what's modern? Yes, they say. Our goal was to be one of the three chains that popped into someone's head whenever they wanted to shop – and to always offer the newest thing. Because if you frequently offer what's new, you'll get frequent visits.'[2]

It is Gina Tricot's first day in a new market – and it should be treated like the last. Tomorrow and the next day and the next will see deliveries of new clothes. New colours, new models – all the latest rage. The brain behind Gina Tricot is well dressed, focused and relaxed as he talks. Shrewd, too, when it comes to business. After 25 years at JC – another Swedish bargain fashion chain – he resigned his position as vice president in 1996 and travelled around Europe to study clothing stores. He counted the items the stores had on display. He noted how much they sold. He watched how customers moved around the store and what they bought. With mathematical precision, Appelqvist registered everything he saw and in his head a new business idea grew – a masterplan that would secure his place in the upper regions of Scandinavian fashion. Eleven months after Appelqvist left his office at JC he opened his first twelve Gina Tricot stores in Sweden.[3] On the day in 2007 that the girls went bananas in the new store, he had a total of 70 stores and 20 million visitors a year. Two years later Gina Tricot had also entered the Danish and Finnish markets, and in 2009 the chain had over 80 million visitors. The time had come to conquer yet another country. In 2010 it was Germany. Today Gina Tricot has a turnover of more than 2 billion Norwegian krone (£175 million/$275 million) and, in addition to its online store, the chain has around 180 stores in five countries.[4] Appelqvist's masterplan was a success. Those crazy girls have made his bargain fashion chain huge and profitable.

A shopping bomb exploded in the wealthy parts of the globe. Within a seventeen-year span – from the day I moved away from home until the day I got married – clothes consumption in my country doubled.[5] And clothing prices fell by more than half.[6] The 2000s were extreme. In just five years – from 2001 to 2005 – clothing consumption increased in Britain by 37 per cent.[7] The number of clothes sold in the U.S. increased by as much as 73 per cent.[8] For example, the Swedish chain H&M opened an average of twenty new stores every year that decade in the American market.[9]

The cause of the explosion was fast fashion – cheap fashion's entrance and enormous growth: chains that stock bargain items and snap up the latest trends, designers, producers, distributors, and then sell their products in a flash. H&M, Zara, Topshop, Gap, Mango, Banana Republic, Target, Primark, Marks & Spencer, Uniqlo and Forever21. They are huge and global, not to mention so numerous and established that if you want to buy an article of clothing today, chances are you will end up in one of these chains. Cheap fashion stores have achieved a market position that ensures they are fundamental.

The philosophy behind fast fashion is simple. Every time customers stick their noses in the door they should see something new. That equals more frequent visits and more purchases. As a result, every week is a new fashion week, and many stores receive new wares every single day. When it comes to bargains, it is only possible to earn money if you produce and sell a lot. High volume is mandatory. And if they are to sell, the garments cannot cost an arm and a leg. It must be possible to buy a new top on the way home from work, even if there's no time to try it on. And if it doesn't fit, a few bucks for a T-shirt isn't the end of the world. Of course, fast fashion chains also make a profit off low prices by forcing production costs down. They locate their production in countries with cheap labour; where wages are low and workers have few rights. The materials can't be too expensive either. So clothes don't last as long as those with a higher material quality. This further increases the demand for new items. Because if fast fashion allows two things to be plus-sized, it is sales figures and customer demand. The need to buy, own something new, exchange and recreate oneself. Without that the business would be null and void. And so fast fashion chains must perpetually generate, feed and cultivate the demand that drives customers to shop. They must perceive their customers' innermost wishes and serve them up at the right time. They must create an accessible version of that which is currently considered chic. And when creating what is new, they must also ensure it is recognizable.

Give people what they don't know they want, and you will get something back.

What 25 years ago was a handful of cheap fashion outlets located in big cities that drew flocks of out-of-towners have propagated and spread themselves to neighbourhood shopping centres. Internet shopping fills up the small market gap that remains. Fast fashion brings fashion to the people, and the people have made fashion a goldmine. The idea was essentially that dress items should be accessible to more than just the few. Items of dress and adornment could actually be created for and bought by the majority. Beauty's tyranny could be a democracy.

Once it was the exclusive right of the rich to be fashionable. Until the 1600s various dress laws prescribed what Europeans could wear. The laws were based on social class and it was strictly forbidden for those further down the hierarchical ladder to imitate what those who loomed above them were wearing.[10] It was only with industrialization in the 1800s that the visual wall between poor and rich, occupation and familial origin, began to crack. New technological advances made it possible to produce greater volumes over shorter periods of time and to transport goods across long distances – even to the other side of the world. Ironically, it was exclusivity itself that paved the way for the numerous and cheaper wares.

Haute couture, the luxury segment where each unique garment is sewed by hand, made an entrance in the mid-1800s. Then as now, its customers consisted of the economically powerful and cultural elite. And since fashion as yet had no other form of purveyor, these haute couture customers came to define what fashion was, thereby making fashion synonymous with high prices and exclusivity. In fact, the hand-sewn garments were of such high quality that each individual part had its own experts. A bodice might be composed of up to seventeen different parts in order to achieve the perfect fit. The centre of this high art form was Paris.

Nonetheless, the first haute couture designer to make it big was British. Charles Frederick Worth supplied his creations to royalty and aristocrats throughout Europe. When Alexandra, the Princess of Wales, was getting married in 1866, it was naturally Worth who designed the dress. Indeed, he was so innovative and modern that he indicated the direction for fashion 30 years into the future. By 1870, Worth's fashion empire had grown to such an extent that he had 1,200 employees and his name was a recurring feature in American *Vogue*. Worth dared to dream big and he saw the economic potential that awaited him on the other side of the ocean. He loaded his dresses aboard steamers and shipped them off to America and Australia and the fine department stores there. On the one hand, Worth was the exclusive and fashionable designer for the few. On the other, he was a hardcore businessman who dispersed his art to multiple continents and gained publicity by outfitting famous artists such as Sarah Bernhardt. He used popular culture as a window display for his work. In this way, Worth reached out to a new group of people: the middle class.[11] Consumer society was born.

At the beginning of the 1900s, new laws were enacted in several European countries that established working hours and the right to holidays. These laws helped strengthen fashion's position. A substantial group of people suddenly had something called free time. And with a greater variety of social activities came the need for more forms of attire. Corsets and long dresses were not suitable for tennis. The beach was not enjoyable in a white collar. The wardrobe needed a greater spectrum of clothes designed for different purposes. The First World War also turned Europe – not to mention the social hierarchy – on its head. On the far side of the battlefield a new era awaited women. In several countries women won the right to vote and some entered the workforce. And a new star appeared in the fashion firmament. Her name was Coco Chanel.

The truth about her has probably never been told. And for one simple reason: Chanel took it with her to her grave. She was a master at spinning stories about her exotic childhood in Auvergne, where she was brought up luxuriously in the country by rich aunts, and other fantastic and completely fabricated tales. Coco Chanel deliberately obscured her life. To date the most likely version is that she was born out of wedlock, that her mother died when she was twelve and that the rest of her childhood was spent in a cloister. Her clothing was easier to grasp. When Chanel was discovered during the First World War, her design proved a revolution in simplicity. The wealthy British polo player Arthur Edward 'Boy' Capel was Chanel's lover at the time. He bankrolled her first store and it is said that his masculine and athletic style influenced Chanel. Her dress clothes were inspired by sports attire – both women's and men's. And Coco Chanel did not take social class into account when she designed. She outfitted rich women in striped sailor shirts, a garment usually reserved for seafaring men from the lower classes. She was also the first haute couture designer to create functional women's clothes. She simplified, reformed and made dressing down the new big thing. Thanks to Chanel, working class simplicity became a form of elitism.

Artificial jewellery was as good as the real thing in Coco's universe and she introduced an entirely new type of multi-purpose outfit: the little black dress. Small, black and simple, women could use it on any occasion.

'You can no longer tell a shop girl from a duchess', advertised Jaeger, the British fashion manufacturer.[12] With Chanel at their head, 1920s designers shuffled the visual codes. In 1929 Chanel and two other fashion houses in Paris introduced a new form of manufacturing they called prêt-à-porter, or ready to wear. These were mass-produced collections that came in standard sizes, leading to a shift in the power structure. Haute couture was no longer an autocracy that determined everything. Now it was factory-produced fashion that overtook the market.[13] Coco Chanel was perfectly clear that she was no artist. Fashion for her was purely business. And a business it remained.

Chanel did her part to transform the French fashion industry into the fifth-largest in the 1920s.[14] However, she did not follow fashion into its budding democratization phase. Haute couture designers had sown the seed in the 1800s and Chanel had watered it. She had broken fashion free of the aristocracy and made it accessible to a larger group. She had updated fashion to something that was in dialogue with its time. However, when the 1960s came around, she was not willing to go any further. Jeans and miniskirts were in and Coco Chanel hated them. Who knows if she ever realized that she herself had laid the foundation for what was to come, that she had played her part to create this monstrosity. For the next nine years Chanel lived in utter seclusion – in fashion's shadow.

In London a new generation of designers graduated from art school. They did not just want to design clothes: they wanted to take on society, challenging ways of living and modes of thought, and to create new and freer ideals. The years of Swinging London had begun. These years saw the rise of both a youth revolution and a fashion revolution – an event dubbed 'youthquake'.

At the quake's epicentre was the designer Mary Quant. In 1955 she opened her shop Bazaar in London. Back then there were no clothes specifically made for young people – clothes in which they could look modern, be sexy and move in comfortably. So Quant designed garments using strong colours inspired by baby clothes, accomplishing her designs with a playfulness none had previously dared display. Until then, British fashion designers had made clothes meant for established and wealthy socialites. Now Quant snipped the hem off the skirt. And there, on the upper thighs, was the key to why exactly Quant's clothing became youth fashion. The screaming colours were one thing. Suburban housewives could possibly live with that. However, a skirt that revealed most of the package, almost up to the crotch? It was too revealing for mature women. Quant's stroke of genius was to create a physical barrier that excluded the adult segment with their cellulite and flabby rumps. Miniskirts were meant for young, unblemished bodies. Quant created a whole new look that became iconic for the 1960s: the little flashy dress, the short boyish hair and black-lined eyes with thick lashes.

The fashion industry now required a new way to produce clothes. The fact that fashion had acquired a new target group who could not buy haute couture or ready to wear from Paris meant that clothes had to be manufactured in a cheaper and more effective way. Youth was the new ideal and the fashion industry had to follow up. They began to make cheap fashion.[15]

At the time, youth fashion and popular culture entered into a closer symbiosis. When music and art took a new direction, fashion followed and vice versa. Within Barbara Hulanicki's store in London, you could physically witness this interaction. Biba, as her shop was called, opened in 1964 and was a decadent art nouveau/art deco-inspired boutique with the very latest in miniskirts, velvet suits, feather boas and unisex T-shirts. Biba was less expensive than Mary Quant, and that made Hulanicki's store a mecca for fashion-conscious youths. At the same time, the store was also a hangout for megastars like Mick Jagger, David Bowie and Marianne Faithfull. According to Hulanicki herself, Biba was at the time the most frequented site in the British capital after the Tower of London. In fashion history, Biba is remembered for casting the mould for the fast fashion industry today. The '60s model Twiggy, who was an avid Biba-goer in her time, believes that present-day Topshop could not have existed without Hulanicki. Hulanicki's straightforward explanation of Biba's success is that good design can also be cheap. There is no contradiction there.[16]

Ordinary people were no longer willing to stand outside looking in. They wanted the opportunity to participate in the fashion circus and become a part of the fashion show. The man on the street no longer needed to blow a month's pay on two garments to be considered a fashion lion. The fast fashion industry expanded and opened the fashion market up to the people. Now all that remained was to shop, shop, shop.

Why Fashion is for the Few

Politically speaking, fashion history is a story told from the left.

In true social-democratic spirit the walls between the social classes have slowly but surely been torn down. In the years after the war, Norway's acclaimed prime minister Einar Gerhardsen lived in a small apartment in a working-class suburb in Oslo while governing the country. A photograph of the prime minister at home in the kitchen while his wife pours coffee and his son looks on has become symbolic. The kitchen is so narrow and small that there is no room under the table for the prime minister's legs; his back rests against the kitchen cabinets behind him. It looks just like any normal family whose kitchen is too small. However, Einar Gerhardsen was also the most powerful man in Norway and would soon enter history as *Landsfaderen*, the Father of the Country, and one of the most notable prime ministers of modern times.

The coffee-drinking Gerhardsen suffered no loss of power and status by being completely ordinary. Power and status can in fact be strengthened by descending the throne and mingling with the masses. And that is just what the head designer for the fashion house Chanel, Fendi and Karl Lagerfeld did.

The underwear campaigns for H&M, with billboards plastered around cities featuring women wearing nothing but, had worked for years. The most successful campaigns even resulted in multi-vehicle collisions. In 2004, however, H&M was ready for something new. The brand invited the renowned fashion designer Karl Lagerfeld to create a collection for them. After Coco Chanel's death in 1971, the house of Chanel nearly went under. Lagerfeld – with white hair pulled into a ponytail, sunglasses and a seemingly perpetual black-and-white ensemble – saved Chanel's legacy and again saw the label placed among the stars.[17] Therefore, much ado was made when Lagerfeld descended the throne and agreed to collaborate with something as cheap as a Swedish fast-fashion chain. Suddenly, King Karl himself was going to design clothes for the ordinary – and even the plus-size.

The commercial for the collection was a dramatic, hyperbolic, pompous and ridiculous record of original Chanel customers' reactions on hearing that Karl had switched sides. These heavily made-up parodies howl, fuss and nervously sip from crystal glasses while Lagerfeld, cooler than ever, calmly replies that it is not about price. It is about taste.

The collaboration was not merely profitable – it was historic. Since the 1800s, haute couture art had been reserved for the few. Two hundred years later the fashion houses still had the scent of luxury about them – and Chanel was perhaps the most perfumed of all. Lagerfeld subsequently distanced himself from the collection; after all, it has been produced in sizes as large as 42. However, H&M continues to follow their recipe for success. Every year the bargain chain launches a new collaborative collection from a new star designer. And each time that happens, a new king or queen clambers down from the throne and goes out to greet the masses.

Stella McCartney, Roberto Cavalli, Jimmy Choo, Comme des Garçons, Matthew Williamson, Sonia Rykiel, Versace, Marni, Martin Margiela . . . When it came time for Lanvin designer Alber Elbaz to design dresses for under $150 in 2010, he justified his guest appearance by remarking that haute couture and fast fashion were just two sides of the same coin. 'Couture is not red carpet. Couture is a laboratory. And without what we do we cannot recreate the fast fashion', he said.[18] According to Elbaz, haute couture and fast fashion cannot live without each other. One is the guinea pig that acts as the frontrunner, the other the whole pig farm following behind. Cheap and expensive are part of the same planet, and therefore it is nothing for him to descend to the people for a brief instant, even if he belongs to the exclusive side.

Star designers do not continue to work in the cheap section, however. They guest star with a limited collection that sells out in a few weeks. After that the designers return to their fashion houses. The arrangement, therefore, is just a temporary social democracy that dissolves when the warehouses are empty. It is like the feudal landowner who tosses a hoe over his shoulder and tills with the peasants for a day. Afterwards, he goes home and the social hierarchy returns to normal. So it is with star designers. In order to glitter, they have to remain in the heavens most of the time. The stars like to say that it is a new and exciting challenge for them as artists, and so on. But the H&M collaboration is simply good advertising. Such a well-known and widespread chain enables the fashion folk to reach people they would otherwise never have dreamed of reaching. The generous part of the concept is the desire to sell a bona fide Lanvin or Versace to a variety of different people. The caveat, however, is that these shoppers must live near to one of the few select stores carrying the temporary limited collection. As a result, it is the thought that is democratic at its core, not the practice. The idea of a flat structure that enables supermodels like Kate Moss to pluck a favourite outfit from their home walk-in wardrobe and produce copies for Topshop so that everyone can look like her is certainly sympathetic. The notion that more customers are better than few is also an inclusive concept, making it natural that Narciso Rodriguez designs for both the first lady of the United States and the Swedish bargain fashion chain Lindex. Otherwise, this democracy is bought and paid for. Nonetheless, the movement on and off the throne does carry the important signal effect that everyone is good enough for fashion, and that economic barriers to looking good need not exist. Blurring the boundaries between expensive and inexpensive has become so respectable that even top designers can walk around in cheap T-shirts from Gap and admit it without blinking. To dress down while dressing up is no longer self-contradictory.

Dressing down entered fashion after the financial crisis hit in 2008. Slowly but surely people grew used to the concept that life would not be what it had been. Many people could no longer afford to buy as much – their only choice was to relax, appreciate what they had and forget the things they could not have. The post-war 'make do and mend' philosophy again crept into people's consciousness. Darning socks, re-sewing articles and self-making things became trendy. British *Vogue* saw the direction in which their readers' thoughts were turning and introduced the old 'More Dash than Cash' column from the 1970s. Here it isn't about showcasing haute couture for thousands of dollars, but inspiring readers to create high fashion from things that are inexpensive and used. In their ads and fashion series *Vogue* continued to be a display window for luxury products, but in 'More Dash than Cash' they ripped the arms off old suit jackets, painted rubber boots new colours and coupled flea market finds with fast-fashion items for a super-trendy look.

That autumn the stylist and designer Shona Heath was given free rein in the column. She created a haute couture look from clothes pins, kitchen towels, washing-up gloves, face cloths, rubbish bags and other things found at home in the kitchen cabinet. Among other things, Heath wanted to recreate the vibe of a romantic Chloé dress. It was made from two packs of napkins, a pack of muffin cups and a plastic tablecloth.[19]

Heath's kitchen bonanza illustrates an ultimate levelling of the old fashion hierarchy. The medieval rules dictating that select is for the select and middling for the mediocre were now gone. After all, when a luxury broker like *Vogue* gets down on its knees and roots through the kitchen cabinets, the barbed-wire fence between classes is gone. After something like that, everyone is free to move about, steal each other's styles and grab whatever they have to hand – cheap, expensive, new or used. That was the ultimate sign that the fashion world was completely democratized. Fashion had come free of its restraints and the market was an arena where anything goes. Now it was just a matter of dressing oneself. Or was it? The 'More Dash than Cash' initiative was like the coffee-drinking Gerhardsen at home in the kitchen – a sympathetic and politically correct gesture. In reality, however, it is completely impossible for ordinary people to transform a set of yellow rubber gloves into a supercool bolero. Most people can purchase fashionable clothing from fast-fashion retailers, but few are capable of combining things to such an advanced degree as Heath and other professional stylists do. It is here that the Robin Hood story ends. For parallel to the growth of fast fashion emerged a more advanced form of styling. The way one mixed clothes, shoes, make-up, jewellery and hairstyles became more important. Now it was no longer about having the right labels, colours or cut. What mattered were combinations, styling, vintage and uniqueness. When the door was opened to all, fashion became horribly complex. Only those who were both fashion-skilled and fashion-conscious could master such an advanced style.

Fashion's 200-year-long democratization process had apparently ended in a surface democracy whose possibilities at first glance may have seemed equal. But beneath the surface an elite still ruled the day.

THREE

Dictatorship

Why Anna Wintour Gets to Be Nasty

Those who think Anna Wintour is teetering on her throne tend not to say so out loud.

Those who applaud her tend not to do that too loudly either. American *Vogue*'s editor-in-chief is one of fashion's most powerful people. Wintour presides over the editorial and visual content of one of the largest and most notable fashion magazines on the globe. She can slaughter the world's leading designers if they offer her a private preview of their next collection. She can sit still on the front row of a fashion show and ensure the designer a career just by being there. In fact, it seems like Europe's fashion weeks set their dates by Wintour's calendar. At her home office in New York City she invariably controls her subjects with an equally brutal hand. In a righteous world, *Vogue*'s proprietors would have shown the woman the door long since and the industry would simply have dismissed her as an overly ambitious child. However, this is the fashion world. The fashion industry may grovel before Anna Wintour, but Wintour grovels before no one. The myth of the power-hungry Anna Wintour is the myth of fashion itself.

In the American TV series *Ugly Betty*, there is no one who wields brutality and Botox like the editor, Wilhelmina Slater. She considers the fashion magazine *Mode* to be her own personal venue and would rather step over corpses than lose one ounce of authority within the walls of her designer-white office. However, she's not alone. The magazine's employees are no Mother Teresas either. The editorial office is full of ambitious, self-centred, wafer-thin, superficial individuals with two things in common: 1) they all want to look better than good; 2) they all want power.

One day, the magazine's CEO hires Betty, a rather plump, bespectacled girl from Queens with blue braces and a pounding heart. So begins the war between good and evil.

The same description of life at a fashion magazine is found in the book and film *The Devil Wears Prada*. Here it is Miranda Priestly who is editor-in-chief of a large and influential publication. And of course she tyrannizes everyone and everything around her. In fact, it would be hard to find a more spiteful and despicable boss or more downtrodden employees. The book is fiction, but it is based on the author's own experiences in the magazine industry. Unofficially, it has been observed that Priestly is Anna Wintour – and at the film premiere the woman herself appeared wearing Prada.

After twenty years in the boss's chair, Anna Wintour allowed a film crew into *Vogue*'s editorial office to document work on the record-breaking September 2007 edition. The documentary *The September Issue* describes a reality that conforms in surprising ways to much of the myth. The film begins with Wintour alone before the camera. 'I think what I often see is that people are afraid of fashion', she says. 'Because it scares them or makes them feel insecure, they put it down.' 'On the whole, people who say demeaning things about our world, I think it's because they feel in some way excluded, or not part of the "cool group". So as a result they just mock it.'[1]

Wintour blames the fashion world's exclusionary characteristic on the people who stand outside of it. She doesn't represent the culture as flawed, nor fault the industry for taking a form that intimidates ordinary people. But it's clear from the documentary that those around Anna are terrified.

There are, however, moments when Wintour reveals a more intimate side of herself, such as when she gives her daughter a soft and motherly gaze. Perhaps she does occasionally betray for a split second that she isn't particularly good with emotions and it is perhaps for this reason that she uses domination techniques to control everyone and everything.

In the film, André Leon Talley, Wintour's then right-hand man in all matters fashion, schlepps his enormous body around a tennis court while his trainer cautiously calls out positive encouragement. The ground Talley manages to cover is not large. He is no athlete. Instead, it is fashion that sets his heart pounding. So why is he taking private tennis lessons? 'Ms Wintour inaugurated me into health. She saved my life, I guess, in the long term', he explains from a bench after the training session. 'Naturally, what Ms Wintour says goes, so I took up tennis.'[2] Sitting there, Talley is almost completely outfitted in Louis Vuitton. The small tennis bag is a dark brown Vuitton with beige monogramming. His skull cap is Vuitton. And the large towel slung shawl-like around his neck also comes from the French fashion house. Proudly, he proclaims that his pants are Damon Dash, his shirt always Ralph Lauren, and the diamond-encrusted training watch a Piaget from the 1960s. Talley may be a fish out of water when it comes to chasing tennis balls, but the things he has on are like moorings to his last remaining shreds of dignity and identity.

Why does André submit himself to whatever Anna says? Why does *Vogue*'s editorial staff swallow her mercilessness without offering resistance? After all, they follow orders that are at odds with their own convictions. Heads bowed, they sit at their desks and lick their wounds. Why don't they stage a mutiny? Most moody teenagers face parental resistance before they can develop into despots. Why does no one stop Anna Wintour?

Wintour was the first to mix expensive design with jeans and to feature celebrities on the magazine's cover. She has an instinct for what is coming and what sells. Because of her, *Vogue*'s proprietors make a profit and occupy an important market position. Still, there is something else at work here – something that ensures that dictatorship and hierarchy are more acceptable in the fashion industry than in others. It is something found in the nature of fashion itself.

Why Fashion is Right and Not Wrong

Fashion is like an index finger. It indicates what people should buy, as well as how they should dress and look. And people follow fashion's directive. It is like marked mountain trails. Most hikers follow the paths with signs. There is, after all, a silent agreement between fashion and the individual: fashion's job is to point the way. And there is an unspoken clause there stating that fashion is always right. Of course, cheap fashion and blogs from the street where ordinary people are photographed might give the impression that people have participation rights. But the body governing Planet Fashion is dictatorial. Power belongs to the few and its exercise doesn't allow room for too many questions. Where fashion points, people follow.

'Nude is in this year'; 'Update your closet with these clothes'; 'Wear fashionable harem pants this summer'; 'That's totally out now'. Fashion journalism isn't like other forms of journalism. Often articles on fashion directly address the reader, coming right out and saying what he or she should buy, wear and blend. When fashion is the topic, the press's ethical guidelines don't seem to apply. Fashion articles can advertise for a select look, garment and designer and include information on price and outlets beneath the pictures. Editors can even write in the editorial column that such-and-such is this season's 'it' handbag and that so-and-so pants are must-haves. And then come the pictures, brands and prices. This is text advertising – a combination of advertisement and editorial content – and is something that many countries consider to be a violation of the press's ethical guidelines. As a result, this form of fashion journalism certainly doesn't live up to the press's ostensible role in society: to inform, create debate and uncover matters worthy of critique. This is what supposedly transforms the press into a fourth estate and a central player in democracy. When it comes to fashion material, however, reeling off this spring's hot garments and relaying the news that thongs are out is apparently sufficient. This doesn't meet the criteria for an 'estate' – though it is still all about power.

Fashion journalism and Anna Wintour operate along the same lines. Both have a licence to point and direct. People come to Anna's office and submit a proposal or show some outfits they were thinking of using for a photo shoot. Anna says yes or no. Or she inspects the layout and picture sequence for the next issue. Her thumb points up or down. As *Vogue*'s editor-in-chief, it is her job to separate the wheat from the chaff. Time and context are the variables here, but her initial position remains unchanged. Fashion journalism operates in this same way. It is a dictatorship that is allowed to operate within the media. And this dictatorship encompasses readers as well, at least when it comes to reading fashion material, responding to ads or buying as directed. Readers seem to accept the idea that fashion dictates and they must obey. There is even a kind of expectation that they will be steered. If nude is the season's colour, then more people walk around in light, flesh-toned clothes. Fashion purports to have the final say on how people should look at any given moment, and people accept its conclusions. They act as if fashion's answer is always right.

The Flowers' Festival (1914) by the Swedish author and artist Elsa Beskow tells the story of young Lisa, a girl invited to take part in the flowers' great midsummer celebration. Lisa is an ordinary child, but when the flower fairies drip poppy juice onto her eyelashes she sees that all the flowers are actually alive. They are beautiful people with clothing made of petals. The flower people arrive in a solemn procession from meadows, forests, lakes and windowsills to take part in the great celebration. And at the centre is Queen Rose.

> At the top of the garden, Queen Rose was sitting on her throne welcoming all the guests, surrounded by her court – Lady Pansy, Lady Peony, Lady Lilac and Lady Honeysuckle, Lord Crown Imperial and Lord Bleeding Heart, Sir Iris, a pretty little Columbine and two little Daisy chambermaids. 'How wonderful that you all managed to be ready on time,' said the Rose, smiling at them. They smiled back and bowed and curtsied.
>
> 'Play up!' cried the Queen Rose to her musicians, clapping her hands. The cricket, the bees and bumblebees at once struck up a cheerful tune and the Dew-cups and Pea-blossom ran around with refreshments.[3]

Everything is perfect and lovely at the festival's beginning. And then the weeds arrive. Scraggly and importunate, they demand to be included in the festivities. This is the story's dramatic climax. The weeds try to force their way inside the gate. 'We're flowers, too', they shout. Eventually, Queen Rose calms everyone down and suggests that the weeds sit out by the roadside.

'"I suggest," she said to the weeds, "that you sit along the edge of the ditch outside the garden. Then you can hear and see just as well, as long as you sit quite still and don't disturb the party. The Dew-cups will bring you refreshments and perhaps Mr Thistle would be so kind as to stand guard at the gate?"' Queen Rose says.[4] Even though Mr Thistle is a weedy troublemaker, he obediently listens to whatever Queen Rose has to say.

Queen Rose adopts a milder approach than Anna Wintour, but when it comes to decision making they both behave in exactly the same way. The queen holds the power, while beneath her is a hierarchy of underlings who collectively obey her commands. *The Flowers' Festival* describes a society that resembles the fashion world. It is a hierarchy based on beauty and power, where those consigned to the bottom rung are able to watch but not partake on the same footing as others. It reeks uncomfortably of dictatorship.

Indeed, British fashion historian Christopher Breward has found some disconcerting similarities between fashion and fascism;[5] he believes that the two have elements of elitism and Darwinism in common. Both blocs consider some people to be better than others. Both feature a Queen Rose on a throne with underlings buzzing around her. The elite at the top make the decisions; the further down the ladder you are, the less determinative power you have. And beyond the gate – the place for scraggly weeds who have no idea how to behave – no decisions are made at all. Quite literally, some are counted in and others out. And because fashion excludes like it does, Breward argues, it isn't democratic and never can be. By its nature, fashion is only designed for some.

Among other things, Breward takes the lifestyle magazine *Fantastic Man* as an example. In itself, there is nothing about this magazine that screams Mussolini. In fact, the magazine is remarkably moderate, polite and proper. Inside it everyone is addressed as 'Mr' and no one is permitted to use terms such as 'sex'. At first glance, the titular 'Mr' might seem all-inclusive. After all, every man is treated like a gentleman. However, the equality principle stops there because not just anyone makes it in. The men who are described and featured must live up to the magazine's title. They must satisfy the condition of being fantastic. The creators of *Fantastic Man*, Jop van Bennekom and Gert Jonkers, were once asked what a fantastic man actually is:

Jonkers: 'We talk about that all the time.'
Van Bennekom: 'We would've liked to have had Bill Clinton if we could.'

Jonkers: 'But I don't think we could've had Tony Blair.
    He's made a couple of truly atrocious blunders, so...'
Van Bennekom: 'Would we have had George Bush?
    Absolutely not.'
Jonkers: 'I personally would have nothing against
    Sarkozy.'[6]

When not focusing on its fantastically selected men, the magazine's articles take up such choice subjects as the perfect handshake, the best socks and the pleasures of taking a dip in a lake. Not much reveals the fact that in 2001, van Bennekom and Jonkers also founded the upbeat gay magazine *Butt*, which is printed on pink paper. *Fantastic Man* is distinguished, stylish, conservative – and exclusive. The magazine functions as a guide to the codes one might adopt in order to appear perfect. Not everyone, of course, is capable of cracking these codes. Only the truly fantastic individual is able to understand them. For Breward, the elitist concept upon which the magazine is built is also the same idea that governs fashion. Just as the number of stripes on a military uniform indicates a person's level of authority, so too the exterior and interior perform this function in civilian life. It isn't just the fantastic magazine that has constructed a world where the right decoration can give you a boost and get you ahead. It is reality itself. And fashion is the recipe.

How Luxury Becomes Luxury

When Louis Vuitton left home to find his fortune, the story goes that he walked the 40 miles from his home town to Paris on foot. The story says nothing about what he used to carry his clothes, but in 1854 Louis Vuitton started his own travel goods company. It was a success. Today suitcases and bags with Louis

Vuitton monograms are sold as some of the best options for carrying one's things.

The long-standing bag producer has also become one of the world's most famous fashion houses. The flagship store on the Champs-Élysées in Paris is like a castle. Atop the tower the fashion house's initials flash gold. On the ground floor muscle men in suits with bodyguard-like earpieces stand filtering people in. This is no H&M with stuffed racks and lines at the checkout. On the Champs-Élysées, 'stocked' is synonymous with an airy and aesthetic experience. Even the Japanese tourists who have enough Louis Vuitton stores to choose from back home patiently stand in line to shop here. The Champs-Élysées store is considered the heart of the Vuitton empire. Behind the broad backs guarding the door are suitcases and bags displayed like works of art. On the next floors hang the latest from the fashion house's head designer, as well as jewellery and watches costing tens of thousands of euros. The window displays and decorations have been specially created by world-famous artists like Olafur Eliasson. And at the top of the castle the fashion house has its own art gallery – also packed with the most famous names in contemporary art. You will also find the same name-dropping tendency in their advertising campaigns. Venerable old men like film director Francis Ford Coppola and actor Sean Connery do not perform for everyone, but for Vuitton they are happy to sell themselves. The same goes for artists such as Madonna and Pharrell Williams. The old bag maker knows the art of picking from the top shelf.

Luxury Lesson 1: Luxury is About Mixing with the Right People

Just outside Paris, 8 km (4 miles) away in the suburb of Asnières-sur-Seine, stands Vuitton's old family home. This was the family's house from the time the business started up until 1984. Today the house is used for representative purposes. It is said that all Louis Vuitton employees travel here in order to experience the soul of the operation. No one can work there and be unfamiliar with it. Next door is the bag and suitcase factory, which is also included on the pilgrimage. Here they discard two-thirds of the animal when they cut the skin. A Louis Vuitton bag must have no pores, wrinkles or insect bites. Here suitcases are assembled by hand and the sliced edges painted with a hair-thin brush. And the employees polish the metal on the bags with white gloves until it shines like gold. Everything is handmade and everything must be perfect. 'We use the word "workshop" and not "factory"', one of the guides politely admonished during the tour.

> As you have seen, we have many items that are hand-made and it is difficult to say how long it takes to make a suitcase. We know that it takes several days, but we can't say how many hours. Therefore, the employees here aren't told that every day they have to make three handles and eight corners. They are told that every day they must do what they do until it is perfect. That isn't like an ordinary factory. Here it's about art.[7]

Luxury Lesson 2: Luxury Must Not Only be Described, but Staged

The representation room in the family house is the old Vuitton family sitting room. It is a beautiful room. Stylistically, it looks to have remained untouched since art nouveau was the new thing at the beginning of the 1900s. The room still gives the impression of warmth and life, as if this is the nice family room that they still decorate every Christmas. During representation lunches, waiters adopt the same old and venerable demeanour as the room. In their white suit jackets and with their reserved politeness, they seem to be cut out of an Agatha Christie novel.

When the fashion house describes itself, it chooses words like traditional, professional, innovative, modern and creative. Here in the old sitting room, tradition is cultivated professionally. Patrick Vuitton, a fifth-generation Vuitton, participates in these business lunches. He also sees daily to the company's special orders. Accordingly, he is head of Special Orders, the department that designs one-of-a-kind products for the rich and famous. Patrick Vuitton is the man they trust with their innermost storage needs. He knows which French politician has a secret compartment in their suitcase to store pictures of their lover. Patrick, however, will never reveal this to anyone. His suit is as impeccable as his perfectly trimmed moustache. He is professionally present, but doesn't reveal his innermost self. When ordinary people with average salaries find the means for a small but authentic Vuitton bag, it is Patrick's exclusive production that saves the fashion house's name. The Special Orders department assures Vuitton is still branded a luxury. And Patrick knows what luxury is. He knows the codes and he appears to live by them. After all, he is a Vuitton.

Luxury Lesson 3: Luxury Does not Mean New and Shiny, but Authentic, Original and Exclusive

Surprisingly enough, during the presentation lunch Patrick Vuitton tells the guests around the table that he is going to reveal what luxury is. Forget about price, he says. The amount of euros doesn't reflect the degree of luxury. The secret is somewhere else. That is what his grandmother told him. She taught Patrick to fry the perfect egg. First, you need a good pan. Then some good eggs – preferably from your own henhouse. Into the pan, good salted butter from Brittany. When that is ready, separate the whites from the yolks. And when the butter is browned, pour in the whites and fry them until firm. Only then do the yolks come into the pan, right on top of the whites. Then a little bit of salt, pepper and a dash of homemade vinegar. Voilà! Patrick lifts his eyes and looks at the guests. He says: 'That is luxury because no one else here knows how to do it right.'[8]

Luxury Lesson 4: Luxury is Inaccessibility

Luxury heralds quality, perfection and tradition, but the ultimate key to luxury is inaccessibility. Inaccessibility because of price. Inaccessibility because of secrecy. Inaccessibility like Patrick's Special Orders department. As one-time European CEO of Chanel, Françoise Montenay puts it:

> Luxury is exclusivity – it is made for you and no one else has it . . . It's the way you are spoken to, the way the product is presented, the way you are treated. Like the tea ceremony in Japan: the ritual, the respect, the transmission from generation to generation. At Chanel, luxury is in our chromosomes.[9]

Fashion's elitism, as the fashion historian Christopher Breward characterizes it, is based on the same principles one finds in the luxury industry. Just like luxury goods, fashion is essentially created for the few. Fashion is all about novelty and being the first one out; all about being something for which people must strive. Fashion is like holding a wet bar of soap. Just when you think you have a grip on it, it slips out of your hand and comes to rest a distance away. In order for fashion to exist, it cannot be everywhere. There must be something unreachable, inaccessible about it. This means that not everyone can be fashionable. There must be an elite, a spearhead, an ideal, something to show the way to those who follow. It is for this very reason that the idea of fashion as democracy disintegrates between the fingers. An elite-driven enterprise can't be democratic. It is and remains for the few: those who understand the codes and those who know the art of dictating to others.

How Appearance Grants Power

Princess Diana's car rolls through Kensington Gardens in London.

It is June 1994. Tonight, Diana is attending a charitable event at the Serpentine Gallery. She is alone. Her husband, Charles, is going on TV to confess his sins to the British people. He will admit that he has been unfaithful to Diana. Diana steps out of the car in high heels and a black dress, with bare shoulders and hem well above the knees. No one has ever seen her like this. There and then, her little black dress is nicknamed The Revenge Dress.

The British press interpret the dress as a significant statement from Diana herself. It says: How can a man be unfaithful to such an attractive woman? Diana's revenge is not sweet – it is little and black.

British researchers Anne Boultwood and Robert Jerrard took a closer look at the dress. They concluded the same thing. With that dress Diana was flexing her muscles as a woman. The stilettos also sent an important message. Charles was shorter than Diana and for years she had been relegated to wearing flat shoes in order to match him. Now the height of her heels grew synchronously with her freedom. The researchers interpreted the stilettos as an expression of Diana's new and independent identity. She was starting a new life, something she communicated to the world via dress and shoes. Their interpretation was based on a recognition that the body's surface mirrors what is stirring inside a person. As they remark, 'Both the body and fashion are independently related to self-awareness, and the nature of their joint interaction suggests a relationship between the two.'[10] In other words, people can express themselves through what they have on. They can show who they want to be and the position they want to have. Fashion is not merely a powerful economic industry. Nor is it simply a power arena for the fashion conscious. Or a power demonstration between the fashion world and those who are outside it. Sometimes, fashion is also a means to power. Diana's revenge dress regained her power and gave her back whatever dignity she had ostensibly lost as the jilted wife. The outfit gave her power.

When it turned out that Arnold Schwarzenegger had had an affair with the family maid, had conceived a child with her and kept it from his wife, Maria Shriver, for over ten years, Shriver filed for a separation. In her first public appearance after the split, she showed up in a low-cut blue dress with her hair styled in a kind of airy lion's mane. She was a free, independent and still attractive woman. She did not need Arnold's muscles to make her strong. The fashion blog Fashionista celebrated Maria's revenge with a photo series featuring dumped and scorned women who cropped up as tasty morsels right after their break-ups. Via glitter and dress, boobs and hips they gave their exes the finger and told them and the rest of the world that now they were finished with the past and ready for new challenges.

That doesn't mean that bare shoulders and a short skirt are perceived in the same way across the board. In other situations, the same dress might be considered slutty and can cost the wearer power. An outfit's interpretation varies with context. The reaction the Norwegian minister of defence received when he appeared in a light-coloured suit at a NATO meeting in 1993 is a good example. The group picture of Jørgen Kosmo and the other ministers made headlines in the Norwegian press. There in one corner was the Norwegian minister in something that most closely resembled a light canary-yellow ensemble together with all the other powerful NATO men in their dark suits. Kosmo defended himself by saying the weather had been hot. That defence failed. The unavoidable question was how could Norway flex its muscles in NATO wearing a suit reminiscent of a newly hatched chicken. The headlines and discussion confirmed what researchers had already concluded in the mid-1980s: a man in a dark suit is considered more powerful than a man in a light-coloured one.[11] Wardrobe as a means to power is something accepted by the majority.

When it comes to powerful careers within politics, law and finance, dark dress is a must. In the 1950s men who wanted to climb the career ladder were advised to wear dark, tailor-made suits. These projected seriousness, reliability and discipline – traits a perfect employee and future boss must possess.[12] When women entered the business world and stepped into the same positions as men, they adopted the male dress code with jackets and skirts. Nonetheless, they could not appear entirely masculine. Getting ahead required a certain degree of femininity – but not too much. Research has shown that, when it comes to the female body, too much skin and form-fitting apparel reduces the chances for advancement. Women who make their colleagues think of sex lose authority. In this case, Princess Diana and Maria Shriver's recipe doesn't work. On the job, something as seemingly innocuous as a neck scarf can increase the chances of advancement, while a shirt unbuttoned a little too much can stop a career.[13] Indeed, researchers have found that the same difference applies to innovative and conservative dress styles. The conservative style communicates the kind of stability that the business world values. It increases the chance of landing a better job.[14] In *Lederboka* ('Book for Leaders'), whose subtitle reads *The Best Tips from a Headhunter*, Elin Ørjasæter advises women to dress up or down according to appearance. Women who are too attractive distract from the job. Grey and boring, however, isn't the way to go either. A slightly above-average presentation is, according to Ørjasæter, the best bet for a woman's career.[15] Researchers in the U.S. have reached the same conclusion.[16]

Dress code is not a precise science. It always varies with place, situation, position and individual. A doctor, for example, will be regarded as a paper pusher and not a medical expert if he walks around the hospital in a dark suit. The suit will cost him professional authority. A white jacket, on the other hand, will increase it. Musician and political activist Sir Bob Geldof doesn't brush his half-length grey hair when he is meeting with world leaders. Nor does he change his rather outdated striped suit, even though he could afford something new and fancy. Geldof occupies a powerful position in cultural life and in public debate. His random and scruffy style doesn't threaten his position as a respected free thinker.

The recipe for which items of clothing look powerful does not remain static either. When 200 students, entrepreneurs, business leaders and academics participated in a women's networking dinner in Oslo in spring 2011, not too many modest scarves were inserted into open shirts. The reporter for the newspaper *Aftenposten* took a positive view of the initiative. Networking lends power. What drew her scepticism was the women's attire. 'Presumably, they are smart, capable, strong and courageous, but they look like peacocks and dolls', she wrote, subsequently comparing the party to an audition for *Sex and the City* and drawing parallels to participants in Paradise Hotel. 'Obviously, a glamorous woman can be a prominent researcher or a strong leader. However, glamour just as easily becomes a stumbling block both for the message and professional excellence.'[17] The reporter's arguments are firmly rooted in the traditional and scientific ideas governing the relationship between women, wardrobe and power. However, when 200 promising women head to a party meant to boost their careers and nonetheless dress like peacocks, that in itself is an argument that the winds are changing. It shows that dressing femininely is perhaps becoming more acceptable in the workplace. Glitter and heels aren't necessarily the negative they were before – not at a party, at any rate.

Appearance should communicate something regarding the wearer's mastery of a situation. It should show how well he or she understands the social codes. In business life, the suit is still the principal garment. In general society, fashion functions as the measure. People's mastery of fashion shows their degree of success. While the right suit can propel the well-dressed man into the boss's chair, being fashionable aids the careers of people in general. Fashion lends social authority. The art here is riding the fashion wave before it breaks. That means arriving early enough to be among the first out, but not so early as to be completely alone. A person should not stick out too much – she should simply distinguish herself a bit with something innovative.

How Fashion Creates Leaders

Hal Larson is a superficial guy. Although he is no looker himself, he has sky-high expectations of the women he dates. They have to look perfect, head to toe. In the movie *Shallow Hal*, a twist of fate propels Larson into an elevator. The elevator stalls, and while he and the other passenger, a life coach, wait, Hal reveals his views on women. The coach tries to help by hypnotizing him. Hypnosis makes him see people's inner beauty instead of their outer appearance. The better the person, the more beautiful they will appear in Hal's eyes. In this way, the hypnotized Hal ends up falling in love with Rosemary, an aid worker with weight issues. Hal sees her as thin and voluptuous when the rest of the world sees her as fat. Even though Rosemary's G-string could be used as a skipping rope, Hal doesn't see the truth before he is unhypnotized. The film ends on a politically correct note with Hal deciding he can't live without Rosemary even though she is obese. Hal is cured.[18] In real life, not too many people reach the same level of recognition.

The appearance of Erna Solberg, Norwegian prime minister and leader of the Conservative Party, has been a running theme in Norwegian politics. During the 2009 election, a TV discussion panel actually said that Solberg 'clearly had improved what she most needed to work on, namely her appearance and articulation'.[19] As a result, they declared, she would be the election's big winner.

A month earlier, a communications adviser had come right out and said that Erna Solberg was so fat that people would not listen to what she had to say. Her body was like signal interference. 'One thinks: can she exercise control when she has eaten herself so fat? Her weight damages her credibility, and that can cost her votes.'[20] Solberg had been pictured wearing large shapeless garments, with rather untidy hair and a somewhat haphazard appearance. However, in true Hollywood film fashion, the Conservative leader struck back. When the election finally came around, Solberg was looking pretty snazzy: she had a new arsenal of classic blue outfits, her hair looked freshly cut and combed every time she was on TV, and her skin was pristine. The Conservative Party made a good showing that autumn; though this was not down to Solberg's new look alone, it was no disadvantage that she had dressed herself up. Female politicians must not just appear competent in order to get votes. They must also look good.[21] And since the majority of the election campaign takes place on television, the politician's image gets intertwined with their political message. Exterior appearance plays an actual role in a democracy. Within a society, dress influences power.

During the Cold War and amid the hush-hush culture of the time, fashion and design were methods by which to spread ideologies, thoughts and emotions.[22] In 1932 the fascist dictator Benito Mussolini even established a separate state institution to govern the Italian fashion industry. The idea was to create a new Italian fashion ideal that would transmit political ideas and give Mussolini greater authority.[23]

In ancient Egypt sandals lent status and power.[24] In militant fifteenth-century Europe, it was armour.[25] With nineteenth-century industrialization and the means for mass production, consumption became a way to demonstrate one's position.[26] Today the world is capitalistic – a place where money, consumption and appearance, together with the ability to communicate, are rated highly. That can explain why fashion helps you to reach the top. Fashion can tell something about wealth, beauty and the ability to communicate. However, the ideal also tells something about moderation. Food is plentiful in wealthy countries. Time, on the other hand, is scarce. Controlling one's food consumption and finding time to exercise is therefore an expression of mastery, success and power. The sleek, trained and suntanned body equates to what is fashionable. Obesity equates to powerlessness. As a result, overweight people might be seen as lazy, stupid and lacking in self-control. In the American job market, it is more difficult for an overweight individual to find a job. And as Erna Solberg's critics pointed out, they can also lose intellectual authority, even though there is no connection between mental capacity and body fat.[27] *Vogue*'s tennis-playing Talley was an important adviser to Anna Wintour and often sat beside her in the front row at fashion shows. Talley may have known fashion like the back of his hand, but Wintour did not like fat people. She could hide behind arguments about health and fitness, but an obese Talley did not fit into her universe. Therefore, he had to fight to retain power – he had to chase tennis balls. There is, therefore, much to indicate that the unhypnotized Hal is a caricatured version of humanity itself.

British researcher Joanne Turney explains the tendency to be superficial with something completely different from the idea that people are shallow. Instead, she attributes this behaviour to instinct and lack of time. Imagine the following scenario: you walk into a room full of people, but you don't know a soul. Whom do you approach? According to Turney, you will obviously be drawn to the people you think most resemble yourself. You approach those who are nice-looking, who are stylish and attractive. If you have a choice between two people, one who is dirty and scruffy, the other in a well-kept suit, you will choose the cleanly dressed individual – even if he strikes you as a dreary stuffed shirt. This is an instinct everyone has and continuously uses. Indeed, today's social structure and lifestyle ensure that we exercise this instinct more often than we did before. We meet so many different people on a daily basis that we never get a chance to see their 'inner beauty'. We live fast-paced lives in a fast-paced world. We move, work and travel all across the globe. We can't get to know people under the same circumstances as we did even a few decades ago. We are constantly being exposed to images, text and branding, where everything becomes a sign to be read. We would be completely cuckoo if we tried to relate to the world in the way we did 50 years ago. It would be too much to handle. Therefore, we consciously refine and filter out what is not important. The superficial perspective simply helps people to cope with and relate to their environment. As a result, we judge a book by its cover. It is a way to gain an overview and survive in a society characterized by information overload.

Human beings are visual creatures – and when social structure and lifestyle compel them to use that instinct often, the exterior acquires more power. First impressions become extra important – along with whatever is on the surface. Just as the rose in *The Flowers' Festival* is queen of the flowers, so fashion is queen of the exterior. Therefore, fashion is a means to power. Not just among ordinary people, but also in traditional power arenas like politics. Just like in nature where the strongest get to make the rules and the strongest survive. Alpha females and alpha males are the leaders of the pack; they are also the ones who are allowed to propagate further.

FOUR

The Brain

How Fashion Hacks the Brain

The philosopher René Descartes concluded: *cogito ergo sum* – I think, therefore I am. Fashion's version is 'I dress, therefore I am.' If we subjected every one of our choices to analysis we would be exhausted before reaching the doorstep. The process mainly happens on autopilot. It is something we just do. It is something we accomplish every day. Like eating and sleeping. The way we choose our appearance has been compared to how parents name their child. They call their baby Emma not because it is the most popular girl's name at the time, but because the parents like the name and think it suits the little one. Only in hindsight will the parents realize that they acted in tandem with many others and were in fact part of a larger wave. Perhaps they also recognize that the name reflects something about themselves or some wish they have for the child later in life. So it is when choosing an appearance – and the relationship this has to fashion.

'Body-fashion interaction lends expression to the unconscious experience of self, both internally as part of a "selfing" process, and externally by creating an identity to present to others', remark the researchers Boultwood and Jerrard.[1] Fashion teams up with a person's natural identity-creation process. The fashion industry hacks its way in via the communication line between the inner and outer person, and establishes a separate screen on the control board where the images from our different perspectives – or surveillance cameras – appear. It acts like a cuckoo chick and considers itself to be a natural part of the family in a foreign nest. Fashion has negotiated a position that allows it to appear as an indisputable part of our society and the lives we lead. It weaves itself via media and the market into not only the fashionista's, but also into the ordinary person's life. The fashion industry produces the effects people use when they shape themselves in their own image. It provides them with ideas on how they can and ought to look. It also compels people to shop.

The fashion industry milks money from a pre-existing and natural mental process – a process where people are perhaps at their most unconscious and vulnerable. It is here we arrive at one of the most troubling aspects of all. Namely, the fashion industry is able to manipulate people according to its own, and not the individual's, best interests. Seen in this light, the fashion industry is perhaps the era's smartest business idea.

Fashion has real authority over people. It can compel people to consume more than they need. It can compel them to forget such basic principles of justice as a living wage and decent working conditions. It can compel the consumer to overlook pollution and the degradation of nature and livelihood. It nourishes one of the greatest and most fervent of human desires – to be beautiful. Does that mean that people are therefore victims of fashion's influence? No. The French psychoanalyst Jacques Lacan suggests that we are all willing participants in fashion, driven by the need for integration.[2] We want to fit in, therefore we follow the fashion. It is also a matter of human will.

Take the current ideal body image. A rail-thin, but nonetheless healthy, body with a suggestion of muscles. A body that requires fierce training and a strict diet to achieve. Most people will fail at the attempt to obtain it. As a consequence, people can become dissatisfied with their own body and develop a poor self-image. The ideal can accordingly be regarded as negative and be criticized by the majority. The media and the fashion industry are the main proponents of this image. It is they who prioritize it and give it scope, and they therefore receive blame for shaping it. However, an important point here, one that is often forgotten, is that fashion isn't simply a surface affair. It also operates within an individual's inner sphere. It plays an active role in both awareness and identity building, and that means that fashion is not only able to influence self-image, but that self-image can also influence fashion. We didn't necessarily need the media to beat us over the head with the modern controlled body. That image might also have originated in the human brain as a visual expression of the qualities many people currently prize: the goal-orientated, disciplined and strong-willed individual.

Take a look at history. The ideal body was not always the shapely beansprout. The hourglass body, women with a boy's figure, tanned men, bulging muscles, slender male bodies, fat women, small breasts, large breasts, long legs, big eyes and bleached eyebrows have all at various times been idealized. The only ideal physical attribute that seems to persist unchanged is that men ought to be taller than women. Otherwise, the body is a piece of Play-Doh to be shaped and dressed according to the day and age in which it exists.

> The actual content of the dress concept is the human body. Fate rests with the body. There are not only people with large heads and slender limbs, with broad shoulders and narrow hips, with high chests and wide behinds. There are also those who have and desire the exact opposite. And if one's body does not fit one's clothing, then the body is reformed. The fixed Archimedean point is neither the body nor the clothing. It is fashion.[3]

So wrote the Danish art professor Rudolf Broby-Johansen in the book *Body and Clothes*, published in the 1950s. It might sound as if Broby-Johansen is saying that fashion is the only solid basis here. However, that is not synonymous with the notion that fashion remains unchanging. On the contrary, fashion is the only sure proof that everything is mutable.

The desire to shape oneself is constant. The desire to imitate the ideal physical image is constant. The desire to earn money in the fashion industry is constant. What varies is the ideal. Why is that? Simply because the picture shifts along with society's ever-shifting current of thought. Thoughts that belong to individuals themselves.

In antiquity, the Greek ideal was a sound mind in a sound body. Draped garments naturally conformed to the body. When the painter Peter Paul Rubens painted the ideal female body as plump and round in the 1600s, he was reacting to the war that was currently raging. Lean times fostered the ideal of the well-fed woman. After the French Revolution, people threw out their corsets. A more democratic garb was now on its way. New classicism's emancipatory Jane Austen dresses, with their high waists and ample breathing opportunities, were in. The ideal always follows from people's thoughts, ideas and reflections over what is happening around and to them. Fashion is essentially a response to whatever is occupying people at the time. A visual response that both reveals and expresses human beings as the social creatures they are.

It is to this that the fashion industry responds. It eavesdrops on the communication line between people's inner and outer selves. It watches and interprets what is happening within and to us and transforms it into big business. People are not fashion's victims, and fashion is no lackey that serves the people. There is a symbiosis between them, like in lichen; which one plays the fungus and which the algae isn't important here – it is the dualism, the interaction, the involvement, but also the shared responsibility that the relationship implies. Both people and industry are responsible for the consequences of fashion production and consumption. The entire affair begins with those inner forces and drives at work within the individual. However, it is also a human-driven enterprise that has become so powerful that the resultant system seems to have become a force in itself. Man's small inner demons – greed and vanity, for example – have developed into something bigger and difficult to control. Therefore, the industry appears stronger than the individual and people seem to be fashion's slaves – even if that isn't the case.

The old whizz Bill Cunningham, street fashion photographer at the *New York Times*, has observed people's true role in fashion's formidable weave. 'Hello, this is Bill Cunningham on the streets of Manhattan New York', he says in his hoarse, rusty voice – cracked with age – on the weekly Internet slide show 'On the Streets'. 'And I'll tell you. The men's fashion shows in Europe have just ended, but the real show is right here in New York.'

Well over 80 years old, Cunningham has spent 50 of them as a fashion photographer. And still he cycles the streets of New York on an old bike with his camera over his shoulder. Back and forth he cuts through New York traffic without a helmet. All he wants to do is snap pictures of what people are wearing. Cunningham is a distinct part of fashion week in New York and Paris and has photographed most of the well-dressed stars and fashion personalities over the years. Everyone in the glamorous fashion industry knows Bill Cunningham. 'We all get dressed for Bill', as Anna Wintour likes to say. Nonetheless, Bill believes that fashion is something he discovers while biking. He addresses fashion to the people and the lives they lead here and now. Fashion isn't something that is simply conceived on the drawing board or born on the catwalk. Nor is fashion fashion just because someone beautiful and famous is wearing it. Cunningham believes that fashion is something everyone has and utilizes on the way to work, when meeting friends at a party or just lying on the grass in the park. Fashion is part of life and springs into existence during the moments we live it.

Therefore, Bill Cunningham cycles up and down and back and forth, day in day out. On a warm New York spring day, Cunningham might snap a series of the year's first summer dresses and show how they are being worn. If it is bitterly cold he might examine how people tie their scarves or how New Yorkers fashionably survive the slush and snow. Suddenly, he might compare the way New Yorkers wear high and low heels to the way women in Paris do, or analyse military colours and items as a sign that designers are stuck in a creative vacuum. He might then go on to discover that hats resembling animal heads are popular, or rattle off an analysis as to why men dress colourfully and women wear black. (Answer: men have become sex objects for women.) 'Marvellous!' Cunningham exclaims.

Why are people still represented as fashion slaves and the fashion industry as a dictatorship? One important reason can be the degree of awareness. On an individual level, dressing oneself is an unconscious process. One's identity project is entirely personal, but not something one undertakes in a particularly conscious state. The fashion industry, on the other hand, is conscious of itself. It intentionally creates the things people want – or the things they tell people they ought to want. It has professional seers à la trend forecaster Li Edelkoort, who can predict that rabbits will come hopping along. It has professional designers who are conscious of their task. It has PR folk who know how to sell the goods. All in all, there is a great deal of awareness around what the fashion industry does. People carry out actions impetuously, while the industry acts intentionally. And so it must be. Otherwise, fashion never would have existed in the first place.

As Danish researcher Bjørn Schiermer explains: 'In my opinion, we do not choose to follow fashion. The day people freely choose their things without resorting to imitation will herald the end of fashion's social dynamic.'[4] Fashion will continue to be fashion so long as an imbalance exists between the industry's degree of awareness versus that of the person.

Even Anna Piaggi, who earned a living by analysing and predicting fashion, did not know why she looked the way she did. At least, she did not admit it out loud. 'Oh, all that', she said, and dismissed what she had just spent hours putting on. 'It's all dressing. I love clothes. I love lots of things. But it's just a ruse maybe, a way of avoiding, of confusing people about who I am really.'[5]

At the bottom of a stack of photographs of Anna Piaggi, wearing everything from Elton John glasses to Mickey Mouse handbags, a journalist from *The Observer* found a picture of a woman in a simple tweed skirt and cardigan. Piaggi, who was sitting next to the journalist, briefly observed that it was a photo of her taken in Britain sometime in the 1950s. Silence fell. In front of them was a photograph of a normal Anna Piaggi. The journalist did not say it aloud, but thought to herself: what the hell happened? How did the proper woman in the picture become the blue-haired creature sitting next to her?[6]

The answer is perhaps not to be found in fashion as the language and conveyer of identity. Perhaps it is found in a third function – namely, that dress creates a smokescreen.

Why Fashion is Death's Opposite

The Bible says nothing about strong winds or cold weather when Adam and Eve each break off a leaf to conceal themselves: 'Then the eyes of both of them were opened, and they realized they were naked; so they sewed fig leaves together and made coverings for themselves' (Genesis 3:7). According to the usual interpretation, Adam and Eve, now sinful, are embarrassed by their genitalia, which could be associated with sex. The leaves are meant to provide distraction so that they can think about more than procreation. In reality, however, most people begin covering themselves of their own free will before they reach sexual maturity and certainly before they understand where babies come from. When children reach school age, they no longer want to fly around the beach naked. Younger children don't see themselves from the outside like older children and adults do. They don't make the same distinction between themselves and the world, nor do they place so much emphasis on what others think. But from the age of about six, slowly but surely, the surveillance camera that watches the self from the outside begins to power on. Perhaps Adam and Eve's eyes were opened in the same way. They saw themselves from the outside and realized that they were not perfect. Therefore, they took those leaves and designed humanity's first outfit.

The British fashion editor Isabella Blow was feeling fragile. Nonetheless, she finished the photo shoot and her mood actually improved a bit while the photographer snapped pictures. With her usual dark humour, she talked about her funeral. 'A funeral, done really well, is just like a wedding', she said.[7] The American magazine *Vanity Fair* was doing a piece on British eccentrics and Isabella Blow was an obvious choice. She was loud and came from an aristocratic family. She loved fashion and had worked as an editor and stylist for several fashion magazines, both at home and in the u.s. At the very beginning of her career, she had even worked under American *Vogue*'s Anna Wintour. Blow had a nose for quality and success. She could smell talent. This is how she discovered some of the greats, like Alexander McQueen, Philip Treacy and Hussein Chalayan – discoveries for which she was never given full credit. Instead, what got her the most attention were her hats. No hat was too outlandish and no occasion too trivial for wearing one. She wore hats to football games and while napping on planes. The hat might resemble a lobster or a plastic plate. It might be a model ship or a village of tiny Japanese houses. And on one occasion, with its wings resting atop Isabella's head, lay a dead bird.

Yet beneath the dress was a fragile and sick person. Blow struggled with depression and eventually became suicidal. She supposedly said that hats protected her from other people's kisses and hugs. They delineated a private zone and freed her from unnecessary closeness. On the day that *Vanity Fair* photographed Blow, she was hatless. She had stripped it all down to an item of armour: an impenetrable, heavy, chainmail-like piece signed 'Alexander McQueen'. Protected only by the metal and the warrior spirit apparent on her face, she regarded the camera with a wounded, tired, yet firm expression. Isabella Blow was ebbing out. She had a plan. Supposedly, she purchased the herbicide on the way home from the photo shoot. A few days later she drank the deadly poison. There was nothing that could be done. The dose Blow took was more than enough. Over the next few days her body died little by little. The last portrait taken of Isabella Blow was *Vanity Fair*'s picture of a fragile creature protected and sustained by the garb – her armour.

Blow's last exhibition was symbolic: the clothing that forms a shell around the soft and vulnerable human body; the garb that wards off the sharp sword capable of penetrating soft tissue and crushing every bone in the body with deadly force. In retrospect, it seems that Blow was able to send a last message to her public about what that facade actually is. She transformed herself into Isabella Blow by dint of what she donned. She did not see herself as attractive, but used clothing and hats to make herself as attractive as she could to her own mind. She devoted her life to this process, though beneath that thin shell the real Isabella Blow was hiding – the woman who was tired of being sick, lying in bed and staring at her feet, the woman who was not recognized for her professional accomplishments, who could not have children and who was getting old and, in her opinion, ugly.

Isabella Blow showed that fashion is essentially about man's cultivation of beauty. That beauty has a central place in human life and helps one find meaning when things get out of hand. However, beauty has another important function: to protect the individual and hide the ugly truth. Just as Disney's The Phantom Blot's black cloak and hood enable him to keep his real identity hidden from Duckburg's citizens, so too can dress and fashion be a conscious distraction technique adopted by the wearer. Dress can obscure a truth that could not tolerate the light of day; a truth that is not at all attractive.

As such, clothing is all about revealing and concealing different sections of the body. At first glance, it may seem that there is no system or logic involved here. Fashion simply changes. One season it might be in to emphasize the legs; many people accordingly follow suit and expose them. Other times it might be the midriff or the décolletage that matters. As a result, the focus hops around the body. However, there is a guiding rule – namely, to show what is pleasing and hide what is ugly. The definition of attractive varies with time, but the perpetual desire for it remains constant. Physical beauty is represented as a goal in life and is considered synonymous with success and happiness. It is also associated with competence.

When it was announced that ordinary girl Kate Middleton was going to marry Prince William, not too many questions were asked about her personal qualifications for the position of princess. Instead, Middleton was applauded for her fashion sense. Essentially, she was a British girl without a drop of aristocratic blood. Nonetheless, she knew how to handle herself and smile – and she had a killer instinct for clothes. It worked. Before they had even said their vows, Middleton was pronounced an international style icon. There were even whispers that she might become a new Diana. Kate Middleton dressed like a princess; therefore, no one doubted that she could perform the job of one. Cinderella, for her part, got the royal position when she brushed off the ashes and donned a nice dress. Snow White was naturally attractive with her milk-white and perfect skin, so all she needed to ascend the throne was a kiss. The same was true for Sleeping Beauty – and she was beautiful even while she slept. As it turned out, the most important point on Middleton's CV was the ability to be attractive.

Royalty, it seems, conducts an old-fashioned stage play, exhibiting power, position and participation through a classic costume drama and the correct behaviour. The royal job is a superficial one. Representing a country means employing a number of visual symbols that are recognizable across borders. A beautiful dress and a fine portrait therefore become important components of the royal stage. As such, their performance is measured accordingly.

Even religions that are ultimately focused on inner qualities have the image of a beautiful deity to follow. Buddha sculptures, for example, do not replicate the appearance of the Indian prince Siddhartha as he was 2,500 years ago. Instead, the sculptures show what was considered to be an attractive person in the culture and time they were made. Buddha sculptures are meant to conceptualize the inner goal of becoming an enlightened human being. This is accomplished through casting the figures as physically appealing.

Even pre-school-age children strive after ideas of beauty. Whether chic or cool, the pink clips and backward-facing caps chosen by four- and five-year-olds to dress themselves up reflect what they consider to be appealing. Children transform themselves into what they – and others – consider attractive. Most people don't appear as they actually are – unvarnished, with scars, a gut and grey hair. Why is that?

Beautiful children receive more attention than not-so-beautiful ones.[8] Beautiful people are treated better.[9] Put attractive women up for political election and they will receive more votes.[10] Indeed, researchers have discovered that people even associate beauty with truth. A symmetrical, and therefore more attractive, calculation is more readily accepted as true than an asymmetrical one – even if the symmetrical answer is false.[11] Research has shown that beauty is the ticket to success, an apparent solution to life's problems.

In cultures where women have fewer rights and opportunities than men, furthermore, appearance can be a means to power. There have been many cases of powerful men who prefer beautiful wives putting them at the helm and giving them influence. Imelda Marcos started out as a beauty queen and ended up as the Philippine dictator's wife. Leila Ben Ali, once a poor but beautiful hairdresser, became the wife of the Tunisian dictator Zine El Abidine Ben Ali, a position that allowed her to fill the country's most powerful offices with her own family members. By the time revolution broke out in 2011, Leila and her once-poor family had amassed a wealth constituting 30 per cent of Tunisia's GDP.[12]

As a report from 2011 observes: 'Beauty is strongly linked to womanhood. Many people consider women's "vanity" to be an essential part of women's "nature", though not otherwise dependent on any biological explanatory principles.'[13] Attractive appearance and womanhood are so tightly woven together that they are seen as one. Beauty becomes a feminine quality and, as a result, women are judged by their appearance more so than men. Indeed, according to the theory of the beauty system, status and power are instead what make men attractive and manly:

Womanhood, on the other hand, is tied to the efforts women undertake to make themselves appealing. Unlike manhood, womanhood isn't an innate trait, but an innate lack (of manliness). This lack is offset by partaking in the female beauty system, thereby transforming the woman into something womanly. This explains both why women are never beautiful enough, but instead grow up believing that their appearance always can and ought to be improved, and why masculine power is tied to a veiled and abstract male figure whose body and appearance is de-emphasized.[14]

The beauty system can also explain why the fashion industry targets women in particular. The feminine ideal is not something that is natural and untouched. Instead, the ideal is the cultivated body. Therefore, it is women who require the most help when it comes to dress. Women are the ones who need to go out and shop.

Author Elin Ørjasæter believes that the pursuit of beauty has assumed the upper hand in women's lives, that the enormous job of making oneself attractive is so time-consuming that it actually slows down a woman's social positioning. Once it was seeing to children and husbands and caring for elderly parents that required women to abandon their jobs. Today, it is the beauty requirement that steals time and opportunities.[15]

Agnes Ravatn, a journalist and author, once calculated that she had spent 3,225 hours just putting on make-up. 'This is my cry for help', she wrote:

Can the cosmetics industry please get a grip and invent some make-up you can wear in any kind of weather for thirty days straight? That would free up so much of my time that, aside from my full time job, I could further develop and perfect Homer Simpson's invention: a shot gun for women that shoots make-up into place . . . Oh, how I envy men their infinitely versatile suit. How is it that we, the world's greatest country, haven't been able to come up with an equivalent garment, an elegant and feminine outfit to which we can turn and be well-dressed in every conceivable situation, a femi-dress? Instead, I'm forced to navigate on a daily basis through a jungle of unsuccessful purchases, before finally ending up in the home office. I'm guessing that a third of all sick days stem from wardrobe capitulation.[16]

When supermodel Kate Moss made a comeback to the cat-walk in spring 2011, the event made headlines for two reasons. Moss smoked while on stage. And the cellulite on her rump and the top part of her thighs was obvious. The fact that she was still beautiful and had managed to remain at the top of the modelling profession for twenty years was secondary. Instead, it was the close-ups of her bumpy backside that circulated the globe. The cellulite shock revealed the fact that Kate Moss is human. And it demonstrated that people have become so accustomed to the retouched and unattainable ideal that the demand for beauty has become too difficult to meet. Today not even Kate Moss is capable of achieving this kind of fictitious image with which people compare themselves and for which they strive. Advertisements and fashion journalism offer advice on how we, too, can become like them – the professionally made-up, styled, theatrically lit and digitally retouched models and celebrities. Even 'everyday' snapshots of prominent style icons strolling the streets with shopping bags and coffee to-go can be considered cheats. Most have professional stylists who arrange their ward-robe on a daily basis. Even if one feels a dash of glamour and success with a coffee in one hand and a shopping bag in the other, imitating the image still means pursuing an unattainable concept of beauty. Nonetheless, with the same attractive force the sun exercises on flowers, commercial forces wilfully draw people towards that ideal. That is where the money is found. And as long as people consider being attractive so important, they willingly turn in that direction.

Nothing indicates, however, that the ideal will be replaced by something repulsive. The social advantages of beauty are too great. Physical appearance conforms to a Darwinist model where beautiful alpha females and alpha males come out winners. Even

Fay Weldon, the feminist and author, offered no happy ending when it came to beauty and success in the book *The Life and Loves of a She-Devil*.[17] In the novel, the protagonist, Ruth, has a lousy and unfaithful husband. He has taken up with a beautiful, powerful and rich romance novel author who lives in a tower by the sea. Ruth, for her part, is a shabby housewife with two crabby kids, and is fat and ugly to boot. Finally, Ruth short circuits and comes up with a clever plan to obtain revenge, money and power. She burns down her house and sends the young children to live with her husband and the author in the tower. Then she begins a self-transformation designed to make her rich and successful and to crush her unfaithful husband flat.

In the Hollywood film version, *She-Devil*, the rotund, big-boned Roseanne Barr plays the role of Ruth. She begins the movie overweight and bespectacled with an enormous mole on her upper lip. And she ends it mole-free, made-up, nicely dressed – but still overweight. Though Ruth undergoes a visual change, it isn't a pronounced one. First and foremost Ruth changes as a person. She becomes more secure, more self-aware, a transformation that is reflected by her businesswoman's attire.[18] Fay Weldon's original version, however, is another matter. In the book Ruth undergoes extensive and painful beauty procedures in order to reach her goal. She acquires a new and more attractive appearance in order to get revenge and regain power. As such, Ruth has recourse to the very means the system once used against her.[19]

In Fay Weldon's world, the power of beauty's ideal is too strong to fight against. If you can't beat them – join them.

Why Beauty is so Important

For the British philosopher Roger Scruton, ugliness abounds. Art and architecture is no longer a study of the beautiful.

Michelangelo, Victorian architecture, decoration, naturalistic painting, by contrast – back then a brush stroke could render eyes that radiated lived life and seas of wisdom. Beauty could take one's breath away. For Scruton, beauty could lift you out of the darkness and into a lighter state. Now artists simply want to be provocative and break taboos, Scruton believes. They see only themselves, which they expose in all their detail. Consumer society has overtaken us all. Advertisements have become more important than art; function more important than appearance. Architecture has been reduced to benefits and dividends, and today's buildings provide accommodation – nothing more. The world wallows in ugliness and so Scruton cries a warning. He believes that people are in danger of losing one of the most critical things of all. 'I think we are losing beauty', he says. 'And there is a danger that with it we will lose the meaning of life.'[20]

According to Scruton, beauty has enjoyed a central place in human life for over 2,000 years. If you were to ask a well-educated person about the purpose of art, music and literature in the 1700s and 1800s, the answer would have been beauty. If you were to ask why, you would have been told that beauty is a value along the same lines as truth and goodness. In the 1900s, beauty lost its value. Consumer society changed the perception of beauty and aesthetics. Because what is beauty actually good for? What is its use value? Since the effect of beauty can't be weighed and measured, Scruton believes that people place less emphasis on the experience of it today. This is fatal. Because beauty still means something, no matter how much one twists and bends it. Beauty represents a universal need found in every individual. Beauty is a counterweight to all the world's suffering and shows people that human life really is worth living. The sight of the sun shining through the leaves, the feeling of entering a sacred church space. That small glimpse of beauty can provide new energy and courage on a difficult day. The sight of something beautiful can truly awaken powerful emotions. It is a kind of sustenance, one that balances the mind, strengthening and refreshing it. 'Through the pursuit of beauty we shape the world as a home and come to understand our own nature as spiritual beings', says Scruton.[21]

The Greek philosopher Plato was also consumed with the beautiful. Experiencing beauty could impart the sense of an entirely different world, a more sensual world one can't access any other way. Beauty functions as a link between the human and the divine – that which can't be seen, touched or physically experienced there and then. It imparts a dimension other than the visual. Like when we fall in love. Then a brand new and non-physical space opens between you and the other. A reality occurs that none can see or measure. This is how it is with beauty as well. The flower's message is the flower itself. It can only be experienced through observation – nothing more.

Roger Scruton is a conservative British intellectual who believes that the traditional and naturalistic aesthetic is the correct one. Yet the aesthetic movement that arose in the 1800s, with adherents like the author Oscar Wilde and the artist Frederic Leighton, was also meant to be a reaction against its time. They, too, wanted to flee the ugliness of their day and age. Through art, design, fashion, architecture and even lifestyle, these aestheticians strived to recall the beautiful.[22] The conception of and focus on beauty hasn't been an ongoing condition that has persisted for several thousand years only to suddenly halt, as Scruton represents it. The idea of what constitutes beauty has always been a question with a subjective answer. Contemporary art and more recent architecture can also be beautiful for those who enjoy them. There is no single recipe for beauty. Nonetheless, Scruton makes an important point when he emphasizes beauty's meaning for people. It occupies an important life dimension. A magical feeling can set in when you see something strikingly beautiful. Without knowing completely why, you are aware that the experience endows the moment with meaning. This feeling can be so overwhelming that it fills the entire body. It can bring tears and banish painful thoughts. For some reason or other, people are automatically drawn to the beautiful without even thinking about it. It is one of the unspoken parts of being human. We require food, water and sleep in order to live. A good life, however, also allows for the receiving and giving of love. The question is whether the experience of beauty is also a part of that.

Nonetheless, is beauty really on the wane in society, as Scruton presents it? The philosopher Lars Svendsen says that the contemporary individual tends to pay as much attention to decorating the facade as he does to what is within. So, how can the focus then be absent? There is nothing to indicate that ugliness is the new state of things. Advertisements don't show people who are delighted by dirt, decay and negligence. The latest trend isn't something the majority considers hideous. Beauty is still the measuring unit.

Scruton seems to have forgotten that the aesthetic world doesn't simply consist of art and architecture. Visual culture is greater than all that. It includes all visual forms of expression – including fashion. Even Plato sought beauty in people's faces and bodies 400 years before Christ. Much indicates that beauty's cultivation has shifted from the walls of museums. Our rapid-paced, capitalistic consumer society follows in Plato's footsteps – it seeks beauty in the human body itself.

Deep within the machine that keeps fashion running is an inconspicuous little gear. It is so small and obvious that it is easily overlooked. This gear spins round and round inside, and few give any thought to what exactly the gear does – even though it is so evident. However, it is this small gear that ensures the machine even runs. The gear is beauty – humanity's relationship to and need for that which is beautiful. Without this absorption people never would have dressed and adorned themselves, there never would have been a fashion and beauty industry – nor for that matter an overconsumption of clothing.

There would never have been advertisements linking happiness to beauty. Dress would not have been dress. In a world that lacked beauty as a measuring stick, people would have clad themselves functionally and pimples and long eyelashes would be one and the same. However, that is not the world we live in. Here beauty almost becomes a goal in itself. To experience beautiful things, to surround oneself with them and to look beautiful individually – there is indeed a driving force in people's visual communication and identity construction. Sometimes it even seems as though it's the meaning of everything. That it is a distraction technique designed to shift attention away from life's unavoidable truth – decay and, ultimately, death.

When Isabella Blow was four years old, she saw her little brother drown. Even though she was a small child at the time, she remembered everything from that day. The smell of the flowers, his body on the grass. Blow transformed herself into an artwork, but she was nonetheless never able to conceal the actual tragedy itself. The wound was apparent even through the plaster. 'She transformed herself into this extraordinary creature, but there was always the sense that she was only just keeping her head above water', as one person commented.[23] Here the outer dress is interpreted as the attempt to keep oneself upright and alive.

Isabella Blow is an extreme example of what Adam and Eve did when they plucked those fig leaves in Paradise and placed them in front of their genitalia. But Blow's example is also purely human. Boultwood and Jerrard describe the attiring – or presentation – of ourselves as an attempt to transform ourselves into something that resembles the ideal image. People try to change their actual body into an imagined ideal, something researchers hold to be an impossible task:

> The real body cannot resemble the ideal body, since this is artificially created with imaginary clothes. We must

therefore use real clothes in order to create a similar image. Clothes may be said to become the body we wish to present, and fashion allows us to present the current ideal.[24]

The ideal isn't cellulite, grey hair, fat and wrinkles. The ideal is rather the opposite of everything reminiscent of decay and death. Youthful and unblemished, unscarred by the lived life, free of a multitude of fears, perhaps, most pointedly, of death. In order to resemble the ideal, one must work on or hide the signs that point to the grave. As such, hair gets coloured, the body trained, acne covered up, dead skin scrubbed away, stray hairs plucked and creams employed to spackle over pores and furrows in the skin to ensure it appears new and even. It is the job of clothes to cover up flaws that can't be removed. All this helps the human body approach the dream body, whatever that may be. The ideal itself is mutable and time- and place-dependent. What remains unchanged is that the ideal is equated with beauty. There is a majority consensus concerning what is attractive; whatever ideal is currently applicable is fashion. Fashion is synonymous with whatever people find beautiful at the time. Fashion is the projection of how the perfect person should look. Nonetheless, why do people turn their backs on reality and abandon themselves to that which is virtually unattainable?

The psychoanalyst Jacques Lacan considered a child's first meeting with its own reflection to be a critical moment. When a six- or eight-month-old baby is held in front of a mirror, it doesn't just see any baby – it recognizes itself. The baby understands that 'that is me'. Lacan calls this the Mirror Stage – the stage where individuals experiences themselves as something more than simply an 'I'. You are your own experience of yourself, while at the same time you are also that person there in the mirror – an object you can perceive from the outside.[25] The baby laughs and is proud of this new discovery. At the same time, it heralds a dualistic recognition that will pursue it throughout life. It is the onset of the perpetual struggle between who it is and who it wants to be. Eventually, it begins to compare itself with other people and starts to see that it has flaws. It realizes that it isn't perfect.

Joanne Turney draws a connection between this experience and the way in which people make use of clothes.

> We begin to see that we lack a number of things and therefore we must hide our deficiencies. Clothes enable us to feel better. They obscure the fact that we are all individuals, that we are all human beings who will die sometime or other, that we are all the victims of illness. We are not perfect – we are not whole. However, clothes allow us to present ourselves to others as if we were whole.[26]

Clothes are a distraction technique designed to remove the focus from our flaws. It is like the armour that conceals and protects vulnerable areas, such as Isabella Blow wore in her last photo shoot. It is meant to obscure those parts that are less than ideal.

One of the most common dreams people have is of being naked. Your clothes are gone and you are standing in the middle of a crowd or crossing a busy street without a stitch on. Dreams of being stark naked are generally considered nightmares. For it isn't merely your clothes that are gone – the naked individual also loses face and control. You stand completely exposed before strangers. That is uncomfortable. The naked truth isn't beautiful. Instead, the beauty construction is what is regarded as attractive. The truth about the body is something people hide. When Isabella Blow's mother realized that her son, who lay lifeless on the grass, had drowned and would never wake up again, she returned to the house and went upstairs to put on lipstick. Blow became just like her mother – she never went anywhere without red lips.[27]

FIVE

The Future

How Fashion Became Evil

'I will say something that sounds terrible. We're all going to the gas chamber, and what I'm saying is that it's not a bathroom. We're going to be killed. The human race faces mass extinction', says Vivienne Westwood. The British fashion designer believes that the root cause of our doomsday state is capitalism and the consumption habits of wealthy countries.[1]

Together with her colleague and boyfriend, Sex Pistols manager Malcolm McLaren, Westwood was a frontperson in the 1970s British punk movement. Today she is a world-renowned designer with her own fashion house and the title of Dame awarded by Queen Elizabeth II. Despite that, her political engagement remains unswerving. What fires her now is the environmental movement. She makes large donations to environmental organizations. Even though her business forms part of the system, Westwood speaks out against consumer society.

> What's happening with this system is that the rich are getting richer and the poor are getting poorer, and the only way out of it is supposed to be growth. But growth is debt. It's going to make the situation worse. We have got to change our ethics and our financial system and our whole way of understanding the world.[2]

Today the fashion industry is the fifth-largest in the world, employing around 60 million people.[3] Most of them live in China.[4] Other countries popular with the industry for their cheap labour are Turkey, India and Bangladesh.[5] A woman in Bangladesh can earn the equivalent of less than $1 making 90 T-shirts a day. That means a labour cost of 1 cent per T-shirt. Minimum wage for these women is less than $20 per month. A living monthly wage is around double that. A labour cost of a couple of cents for a T-shirt would ensure these workers a decent life, but the idea behind fast fashion is not for the workers to earn money. In retail stores just one of these T-shirts can sell for about $25.[6] Shoppers certainly save something, but the profits go right to the top – to the owners of the fast fashion chains.

In the Indian clothing industry, only 3 per cent of workers are unionized.[7] In the cotton industry, 300,000 child workers are registered.[8] Because the fast-fashion industry operates with so many subcontractors, it is impossible to control all that happens at each point along the way. Therefore, much that occurs is off the record. The clothing chains might well have ethical and environmentally friendly guidelines and talk about the idea of social responsibility. However, the industry's current production model makes it difficult to have actual oversight.

Cotton is the most common material. It is also one of the most polluting. Conventional cotton production requires immense quantities of pesticides. Even though cotton production only accounts for 5 per cent of agricultural land use globally, it accounts for a quarter of pesticide use. Every year around 3 million people are acutely poisoned by the pesticides used in cotton production. The mortality rate is uncertain. The number is estimated to be somewhere between 18,000 and 220,000 a year. Nearly all of these cases occur in developing countries. In addition, there is high-level use of fertilizers – something that leads to significant levels of emissions of the greenhouse gas nitrous oxide (N_2O) and to soil depletion. Cotton production also requires substantial water consumption. This pollutes the water, reduces biodiversity and contributes to desertification.[9] Nonetheless, cotton – together with environmentally unfriendly polyester – makes up 80 per cent of the world's textile market.[10]

Since clothes are manufactured in countries with low labour costs, the finished products must be shipped over long distances in order to reach customers in the rich West. This increases the emission of greenhouse gases such as CO_2.

A study from 2010 showed that on average British women spend three years of their lives shopping. The wardrobe pursuit totalled over 100 shopping hours per year. That is to say, 90 shopping trips per year – or two trips to the clothes store every week. In addition, there were 60 trips to find shoes, accessories and cosmetics and 51 trips just for window shopping. Online shopping was not included.[11] When the garments finally make it home, the process enters its most energy-consuming phase.[12] The more clothes, the more washing required. And since most garments are made of cotton, that means a particularly high volume of washing. Cotton has no self-cleansing properties, unlike wool; cotton quickly starts to smell of sweat and it is difficult to wipe spots off it with a wet rag.

Today a typical British household has clothing worth around £4,000 ($6,300). Nearly one-third of these garments will not have been worn in the past year. Annually, 1.1 million tons of clothing are cleared from these closets, ending up in recycling, on the second-hand market or in the dump. Half of these will achieve new life, while 350,000 tons will end up in landfill sites.[13] In terms of second-hand clothes, one-third of the world's used clothing ends up in Africa south of the Sahara – countries that in the last decades have suffered recessions in their own textile industries. The importation of used clothing is one of the causes of this.[14]

This food chain dead ends at a cliff. Waste products are not nutrients that can be reused. They are materials that degrade with difficulty; some are even toxic. The energy use of production and consumption and their effect on nature destroys the livelihoods of people around the globe. This chain even damages its own producers. Such a system isn't viable in the long run. Ultimately, the predators at the top will also pay the penalty. On the surface, fast fashion may seem like a just idea that opens up fashion to all. However, it is basically an environmentally unfriendly and inhuman industry. Nonetheless, consumers are devoted to cheap fashion, a passion that seems almost blind.

Still, the dressing game is further dictated by a greater economic game – the game of eternal growth. In the 1920s the world's leading light bulb manufacturers made a deal. They would not make light bulbs that lasted longer than 1,000 hours. By then light bulbs could already burn double that – the technology was good enough. And perhaps for that reason industry leaders saw a dark cloud looming. Because what would happen if light bulbs improved even more and lasted even longer? They needed to limit the bulb's lifespan. That was the only way to earn money. Still, it was not until 1940 that they actually neared their goal. At that point, the quality was so bad that the bulbs were perfect. This pact was the first example of planned obsolescence, an accord based on prearranged errors or functions deliberately planted in a product so that it won't last. These agreements are important in today's global economy – where consumption creates growth and growth is more important than demand. Because to the capitalist mind, growth is critical for growth's sake. Following the light bulbs, planned obsolescence has been applied to a variety of products. Printers have an inbuilt self-destruction mechanism after a certain number of copies. iPod batteries are designed to work for a certain number of months. In the clothing industry, there was an early accord among stocking manufacturers. Nylon stockings were seizing the market, replacing flimsy silk ones. This material was a gift to women, who finally no longer had to worry about stockings unravelling. The first nylon stockings turned out to be so robust that they could tow a car. The producers became anxious that they might not sell enough. Stockings needed to be of lower quality. After all, better holes in stockings than in wallets.

In the 1950s another tool to push consumption forward appeared. Now consumers would not only be forced to buy new things; they would also be tempted to shop. Through fresh design and elaborately planned marketing and advertisement, manufacturers would awaken the drive in consumers to always want something new. They would cultivate the eternal desire for something else. As such, customers would purchase more things more frequently, whether or not they needed them. All these purchases would secure economic growth.[15] Today this system is so established and comprehensive that it is difficult to see how society would ever have functioned without it. Capitalism has become an overarching zeitgeist in a society where the ideology of the right life is synonymous with the consuming life.

In 1992 the writing was on the wall. Manufacturing and consumption patterns in wealthy lands were the chief reason climate problems were under way. This was according to the action plan from the UN Earth Summit in Rio de Janeiro.[16] Already the connection could be seen between consumption and the emission of greenhouse gases into the atmosphere. Too high an emission of these gases – especially CO_2 – leads to higher temperatures. This warming effect will ultimately change the climate, worsen living conditions and cost millions of people their lives. Today CO_2 emissions are around 400 parts per million (ppm). Scientists believe that 350 ppm is the limit required to safeguard our future. That is impossible at today's levels. And if too much time goes by before emissions are reduced, the situation will be irreversible.[17]

In November 2001 the independent organization International Energy Agency issued a warning that the irreversible turning point might appear as early as 2016.[18] The financial crisis had not influenced greenhouse gas emissions at all. In 2010 more carbon was released into the atmosphere than ever before.[19] Together with this warning, the UN's Intergovernmental Panel on Climate Change issued a report concerning climate change and extreme weather. The report was clear on two things: more extreme weather could be expected in the future and the cause was the emission of greenhouse gases.[20] In spring 2014, the Panel followed this up with an even more comprehensive report. As it turned out, climate changes are already occurring – and on all continents.[21] 'Nobody on this planet is going to be untouched by the impacts of climate change', was the grim message from the panel's leader, Rajendra Pachauri.[22]

The desire for new and numerous possessions is ultimately deadly. The guilty party here is people who live in wealthy developed countries. The 20 per cent who are sitting on three-quarters of the world's income. The highest-income earners are the ones who tax natural resources and the environment the most.[23]

It was the books by the British researcher and environmental activist James Lovelock that opened Vivienne Westwood's eyes. Lovelock is most famous for the Gaia hypothesis – a theory that regards the earth as a self-regulating super-organism. In the 1960s the theory was dismissed by many as New Age drivel, but today it forms a basis for serious climate research. Lovelock was also the first to detect chlorofluorocarbons in the atmosphere, a compound that breaks down the ozone layer and increases the greenhouse effect. In 1965 Shell asked a handful of researchers how the world would look in 2000. When they came to Lovelock, he answered that the environment would be the most pressing problem – so pressing that it would affect the oil industry. He was right. However, he now believes that global warming has lasted so long that it has already approached the irreversible stage. There is nothing we can do to stop the inevitable. Certain parts of the planet will become too hot to live or to grow food in; other parts will sink under water. There will be mass migrations, famine catastrophes, epidemics and death. By the year 2100, as much as 80 per cent of the earth's population might have been wiped out. Nature is beyond hope. Humanity must simply adjust to the coming reality, and save themselves through new technologies.[24]

Westwood considers Lovelock a genius along the lines of Darwin and Einstein. However, she doesn't share his pessimism when it comes to taking action. In her opinion, it is still possible to turn the ship around. 'It's presented as though the financial crisis and climate change are two different things, but they're connected', Westwood says. 'We're letting businessmen do what they want. People get paralysed by the enormity of wrong things in the world. But there's so much that one person can do.'[25]

Fashion isn't just a capitalistic project. It is also deeply personal. Human consciousness is where we find the actual cause of fashion's very existence. Perhaps the solution to the fashion problem can be found there, too.

Why Synchronized Swimming is Difficult

The little clownfish Nemo knows a trick. If he is captured by a trawl net, there is only one way to survive. All the fish must swim downwards. If all the fish in the net swim synchronously towards the bottom, the net will drag the boat down. The boat will list to the side, and maybe tip over completely. In order to avoid a dunking, the fishermen must cut the net loose. At this point, the fish can swim out alive and free. In the film *Finding Nemo*, this trick works well. In reality, it is more difficult to implement. A consumer- or manufacturer-driven upheaval of the fashion industry is the only plausible solution to the fashion problem.

Accordingly, people must move in one and the same direction; just like the fish, everyone must act in accord. Nonetheless, we all continue to swim our separate ways.

The problem with fashion is that the original dress system that people practise is woven into the capitalistic system – not to mention into the global economy. Together, the two systems are in the process of wreaking havoc. The consumption of dress items alone doesn't create the problem, but since dressing up is central to the consumption habits of wealthy countries, it forms an important component in understanding the problem and finding a solution. If catastrophe is to be avoided, there is something in these two systems that must change. The facts are on the table. Indeed, the documentation is so solid that even heavyweights like the UN are certain that climate catastrophe will happen and that the high consumption rate in wealthy countries is a main contributing factor. It all comes down to motivation. Some people believe that Judgment Day is at hand and have already given up. Global warming has reached the point of no return. All one can do is enjoy life while one still can. Others believe that there is still time. They lower consumption, make and apply dress in more environmentally friendly and humane ways. Nonetheless, the largest group are still those that do nothing. Either because they don't care or because the problem seems too overwhelming to solve. The first significant obstacle is capitalism. What happens if we do away with it? What kind of a society will we have if we excise what appears to be society's very life nerve? The other obstacle is the human psyche. Consumption reaches deep into one's life and self-image. How can we alter something that is so all-pervasive and that, moreover, happens on an unconscious plane?

According to French theorist Serge Latouche, 'Anyone who thinks that infinite growth is consistent with a finite world is either crazy, or an economist.'[26] He is an ardent proponent of degrowth theory – the absolute antithesis to the capitalistic growth philosophy. Degrowth is about reducing production and consumption, and in this way attaining a more sustainable – and happier – society. In order for this to happen, changes must take place on both national and international levels. People must also adjust their values. In a degrowth society one must find worth in things other than the material.

If we apply this way of thinking to the fashion world, it means that manufacturers must produce fewer goods with better and more lasting quality. Products must be created nearer to the consumer and made with environmentally friendly materials that do not destroy the natural world. People who produce the goods must also have a just and humane system of laws to shield them as human beings and workers. This includes the right to participate in labour organizations and to make a living wage. And orchestrated demand creation – items such as ads – must shift from seductive to informative if they are even to exist at all. In a degrowth world there is no place for fast fashion. Here one shops for quality goods when one has actual need of them. Quality instead of quantity. Utility before emotionally driven want. A humane and environmentally friendly approach instead of an unjust and destructive one. A degrowth society is all about choosing right instead of wrong, prioritizing long-term benefits over those found in the here and now. People must free themselves from the illusion of their own consumption needs. This takes awareness. Therefore, the degrowth individual must fight with his or her inner obstacles.

Obstacle 1: Greed

Greed might be a clever trait when it comes to survival. However, it isn't necessarily a positive one – and in any case not if it is given free rein and allowed to increase. When the individual becomes more important than the collective, greed grows out of proportion.

When the Tibetan Buddhist spiritual leader, the Dalai Lama, visited the European Parliament just as the global financial crisis became a reality in December 2008, he clarified the situation thus: 'Market itself is a creation of human beings. What is the real cause of this sort of economic crisis? Too much speculation and ultimately greed.' The Dalai Lama offered a solution: 'The potential to help is: reduce greed and (increase) self-discipline.'[27]

History shows that people have problems controlling greed, and if some succeed, there are always others who don't. Colonialism was based on the conviction of one's own superiority and the licence to appropriate from others. Capitalism is founded on these same principles. Power is achieved by number of possessions – not by doing what is right. Volume outranks decency. If society is going to scale down greed, values will need to change. Individualism, however, acts as a stumbling block here. One must stop and think in order to understand the total consequences of an action. And as long as the individual is more important than the collective, it will be difficult to control greed.

Obstacle 2: Time

Time is short. The demand for profitability in the workplace has resulted in fewer employees and a greater workload. Internet and mobile phones have transformed communication into something simple and quick. Time is scarce and slogans like 'Simplify your life – find time to live'[28] are interpreted as positive statements. So where is the reflective space for an individual to contemplate themselves from without so that they can act correctly? And where in the world can the individual find the time to track down the right wares, so long as fair trade and environmentally friendly products are not readily available everywhere? And even if the label says 'green' or 'fair trade', it isn't so certain the products are all that favourable. After all, manufacturers have subcontractors whose actions they can't oversee. Therefore, revelations of child labour and toxic environmental emissions that the manufacturer knew nothing about still surface. Is there any point in taking the time to find the right things then?

Shopping is also a quick road to happiness. One's problems can take a long time to fix, but a new dress can provide immediate gratification. Of course, one can obviously repair or re-sew what is already hanging in the closet, or knit a new sweater. Wool from local sheep is an environmentally friendly product and anyone knitting on the sofa has good working conditions. Wool also requires less washing. However, local wool is difficult to locate, and when can any of us find the time for handwork? Living correctly takes time, and if one is to find the time, one can't follow the mainstream. A person might be required to take a less demanding job or reduce their hours and settle for a lower pay packet. However, environmentally friendly products are expensive. One must have money to afford them.

Obstacle 3: Attitude vs Behaviour

You see yourself as a conscientious person who tries hard to do the right things in life. There are recycling containers in the kitchen; the point of life is love and good friends; and before you buy anything, you ask, 'Do I really need this?' You have all the right attitudes, you believe yourself to be a decent and well-informed individual. However, that doesn't actually translate into doing the correct thing. Even if you consider recycling important, toilet paper tubes can end up in the bathroom wastebasket instead of the paper recycling bin in the kitchen. Even if you believe in owning less, focusing instead on the things you already have and that make you happy, you can still buy unnecessary items. You might recognize the connection between the type of products one buys and their environmental effect on the future. However, perhaps the shops that sell those products that are more beneficial to the environment aren't on your current route, so instead you pick up conventional items from an ordinary supermarket. You might say to yourself that you don't need another sweater – there are enough in your wardrobe as it is. Nonetheless, a little voice pipes up and observes, 'But you've never had that colour before.' So you make the purchase. Attitude is not synonymous with behaviour. People do not automatically do the things they think are smart. They might believe they do, but act otherwise all the same.[29]

Obstacle 4: Sacrifice

Shopping isn't just about acquiring things and constructing an identity or attaining a position in society via one's appearance. Shopping is also tied to relationships and love, and can even resemble ritual sacrifice. The anthropologist Daniel Miller observed shopping habits on a north London street for a period of a year. He discovered that buying was not simply an expression of individualism and materialism: people bought food, clothes, shoes and other things for their loved ones. They expressed their love and caring through these purchases. It was like making a sacrificial gift. Miller believes that people do not have a significant consumption drive. What sets the standard is the income of others and the sense of what they have.[30] Behind the consumer is a beating heart. Shopping is about cultivating and conveying social relationships. Consumption is actually a form of human expression.

Obstacle 5: Beauty

After Hal Larson in *Shallow Hal* has been hypnotized and only falls for truly good people, his friend becomes so desperate that he seeks out the hypnotist. He and Hal used to check out beauties together, but now he is alone. In his friend's eyes, Hal has gone insane because he falls for those who are physically ugly. His friend, therefore, wants to persuade the hypnotist to release Hal. At that point, the hypnotist asks: Who says they're ugly? To his way of thinking, Hal has not been hypnotized – he has been unhypnotized. He believes it is society that hypnotizes people into thinking that only a small number of people are beautiful. The definition of the ideal person – the fashionable individual – seems to have clouded our perception. It is this that leads to an overfocus on the surface.

The hypnotist's liberal viewpoint on beauty goes hand in hand with a degrowth society. Happiness can't be exclusively tied to an attractive exterior if dress consumption is going to decrease. However, habits are difficult to change. People take courses to learn to do it. They find groups to motivate and support them to transform their eating or exercise habits. And after the class comes the regression. Monks renounce family, jobs, possessions and sex in order to reach a similar state of clarity. So how can a stressed-out mother-of-two with a full-time job do the same? Even for those who really strive at it, it can take a whole lifetime to change habits and thought patterns – and many times it doesn't happen at all. Insight and good deeds are beautiful golden objects hanging way up high, difficult to reach.

How People Do Good

Hope does exist – in people who take charge of themselves and transform their lives for the good. The author Colin Beavan was perpetually critical. He followed the news, he engaged in debate, he complained, but otherwise he did little to change what he thought was wrong with the world. Finally, Beavan got tired of himself. He realized he was a whiner; someone who took no responsibility. He decided to change: to become No Impact Man, the ultimate environmentally friendly world citizen who neither polluted nor put carbon into the atmosphere. He would live as the future required. Beavan would become a green superhero.

Beavan and his family reduced all resource consumption to the absolute minimum for a whole year. He lived in densely populated New York and here his family would produce no waste, no toxins, watch no TV, use no air conditioning, heating or anything else requiring electricity. Shopping for items of dress and clothes was a no-no. Food had to be grown ecologically within a certain distance from their apartment. Was it possible? Yes. Did it last after that one year? Yes. No Impact Man became the spokesperson for the simple life. He became an avid cyclist, as well as a thinner, healthier and, according to him, happier person. In fact, his entire family life improved by having less. Beavan wrote blogs, books and established the No Impact Project – a programme in which families the world over can take part. That first happy year became a documentary film, and Beavan went up for congressional election in 2012 as a member of the Green Party. He wanted to spread the knowledge and pleasure he had found in a non-destructive lifestyle. An important part of that life, he discovered, was becoming conscious of desire:

> I think a lot about the place of desire. An incorrect relationship to desire, I believe, has got us in this mess. Certainly an incorrect relationship to desire has often got me in a mess! On the other hand, I don't believe desires are meant to be eradicated. Desires are part of the grand scheme. The problem comes, however, when [we] mistake desires for the grand scheme. As though desires are the be all and end all. They are not. They are indeed part of the grand scheme. But they are only a part. The middle way, I think – the challenge – is to find a way to align our desires with the needs of the world. So

that the two come together. If we can do this, then we help ourselves to help the world and help the world to help ourselves.[31]

Designer Sheena Matheiken had no desire for more clothes. In fact, she wanted to see if she could limit herself to a single dress for a whole year. Matheiken specifically designed a number of identical black dresses that could be worn backwards, open and closed. They could be used as dresses, jackets, sweaters, vests – whatever Sheena might want, all in one and the same garment. Every day for a year she would have a different look in the same dress. By turning it inside and out, and by using old, handmade or donated dress items and accessories, she would still appear cool and trendy – without the consumption. However, the project would not just be about her. It would also have a social effect – she would collect money for poor school children in India. In May 2009 she launched The Uniform Project – a blog that showcased her outfit day by day. People all over the world could follow whatever Sheena had on, donate money and be inspired. The girl with one dress appeared in newspapers, fashion magazines, on TV and in blogs the world over. The poor might be limited to a single outfit, but here was a prosperous American who deliberately chose to have less – and looked good doing it. By the time the year was up, her Internet site had garnered over 1 million hits, collected $100,000 for under-privileged children in India and she was named one of *Elle* magazine's Women of the Year. Following in Matheiken's wake, others have adopted the wearing of a single dress for a certain period of time as a way of collecting money for charitable causes. On Matheiken's website they also continued to sell black, environmentally friendly and adjustable dresses in either pre-sewn or pattern form.

The British designer Suzanne Lee also defected from the fashion circus. The industry was based too much on use and disposal for her taste. She did not have the conscience for it. Instead, Lee began experimenting with an eye to the future. Between the clothes racks and cutting boards in her London studio, she filled tubs with tea, sugar and parent cultures of bacteria and yeast. The mixture grew into skin-like flakes, a material she could dry and use to sew clothes. The materials of the future don't necessarily need to be cultivated like cotton in a field. It can also be grown at home in the bath. 'Imagine that you came from some other place and landed on planet Earth today, and you knew nothing about the industrial revolution. You know nothing about how people made themselves clothing and so had to start from scratch. Maybe you would've thought in this direction instead of the way we have produced for thousands of years', she says.[32]

Handling the material is like touching a combination of skin and oilskin. It reminds you of thick, unbleached baking paper. When the bacteria are given something sweet to eat, they spin a network of cellulose fibres that extend in different directions. That makes the material strong – in a wet state it is even stronger than leather. After nearly two weeks the cellulose mat fills the entire bathtub. Then Lee takes the mat and sets it to dry between two wooden boards. This is BioCouture – Suzanne Lee's forward-looking vision and design project. Or biomimicry – which is the common name for the technology. That is to say, the development of products where you turn to nature itself to find new, environmentally friendly solutions. You imitate nature's own processes. Suzanne's goal is to find a resource-friendly, 100-per-cent ecological way to produce textiles from cellulose. A material that can replace the environmentally harmful textiles we have today, or at the very least function as a supplement to them. In contrast to conventional cotton production, the waste from bacteria-produced cellulose pollutes absolutely nothing. You can drink the solution, eat the bacteria – if you want – and the whole thing is so easy to cultivate that anyone can do it. Lee uses green tea, but you can also use other blends. Instead of sugar you can use waste from food production or from factories that pump out sugared water. In addition, the bacteria themselves are, so to speak, gratis and harmless.[33]

There are just a few problems Lee has to solve first. Right now the material absorbs water. A rainfall will swell today's version to a thick, swampy mess. And then the means must be found for mass production. Isolated bathtubs in an office aren't enough. A string of scientists must hop on board to ensure Bio-Couture's future. Clothes made of grown materials, furthermore, won't hang on display at H&M anytime in the next week or year. It will take time to attain the quality that makes bacteria-cultivated cellulose garments an actual alternative. The clothing must meet consumers' demands – just like all other forms of clothing. They must keep the body warm and dry, be comfortable to wear, and do their part to signify an image. It isn't enough to be forward-thinking and well meaning. Clothes are clothes.

Nonetheless, Lee thinks that environmentally friendly innovation isn't enough to solve environmental problems. The real issue is still the quantity people are buying. However, the problem can also become the solution. 'The way to go is for consumers themselves to be selective about what they buy', she says.

> Customers have to enter shops and ask where things are made, how they are made and what happens to the residual waste. You have to ask these questions as a consumer. You're the one with the power to change things. You can spend your money on this or some other brand, and when you make these choices, the brands themselves will begin to ask the serious questions.[34]

The fashion industry has a trigger point that makes it vulnerable and willing to change. People's spending habits can force the industry to switch to humane and environmentally friendly production methods. That is to say, consumers play a corrective role in terms of the industry, and that gives them authority. The power to swim down.

Of course, consumers can also choose to swim in several different directions. We can:

1. continue as before with high consumption and emphasis placed on the same conventionally manufactured products;
2. consume fewer of these conventionally manufactured products;
3. continue as before, but with a larger portion of environment- and worker-friendly products;
4. consume less, and with a greater selection of environment- and worker-friendly products.

Suzanne Lee leans towards alternative four. It directly addresses quantity and methodology, and offers a real solution to the problem. The alternative generally practised today is a conglomeration of alternatives one and three, with three playing a scattered and insubstantial role. We shop like before, and sustainable products are so scarce that they are more like facade decoration than actual contributions to change.

Mary Portas is positive. The British broadcaster, author and fashion consultant believes that something is actually stirring – in Britain at any rate. She observes that fast fashion has caused consumers to eat too many hamburgers, so to speak, and they are now full. The habit of ducking in and out of stores every week, changing to a new look, a new colour, a new style, has got out of hand. Yet what is beginning to happen, she believes, is that people are growing a conscience. They are beginning to consider their wardrobe and ask how much they truly need, with the result that we will see an ethical movement in high street fashion.[35]

Portas makes a living from understanding which trends are up and coming and what customers want. The Queen of Shops, as she is known, has helped to propel the fast-fashion chain Topshop and the department store Harvey Nichols to their current level. She is known for television shows which are suggestive of a crusade against subpar shops and bad service. Queen Mary has a clear formula regarding what shopping should be and what it is shoppers want. 'The "more, more, more" attitude is over', Portas says. 'The G-spot has moved. We're over the greed and the gain. We're over the gloss, the glamour and the hype. Now we want generosity and giving.'[36]

Mary Portas believes three things have contributed to this transformation. The financial crisis has forced many people to consume less and to think more carefully about what they are buying. The threat of irreversible global warming has awakened people's environmental consciousness. And experiences with great customer service online makes consumers want personal service in stores.

Jane Shepherdson was also part of the dream team that made Topshop a fast fashion success. In 2007 she jumped ship and in 2008 became CEO of the British clothing brand Whistles, and now Shepherdson thinks that fast fashion will transform itself into ethical fashion. It will take time, but it will happen. After all, if you spent a couple of pounds on a T-shirt, it is clear that someone else is paying for it. Because whoever made that shirt is probably not making a living wage. And since no one likes to be driven by guilt, people will change their shopping habits. They want to feel good about what they are buying.[37]

Today many fast-fashion chains sell so-called 'green' apparel that is entirely or partially made of ecological or recycled materials. H&M has even given these favourable products their own name – the Conscious Collection. And for the last couple of years they have not only produced individual garments, but have also launched environmentally friendly collections. The emphasis is still on consumption, but the initiative enables people to buy right-minded clothes and it also gives consumers the opportunity to tell the manufacturers that they want to have them. In 2010, Goodone's environmentally conscious designers even created a collection for Topshop. The brand repurposes old sweaters, used T-shirts and textile waste from fashion houses. During a tour of H&M's factories in Bangladesh in 2012, CEO Karl-Johan Persson also issued a demand. The authorities in Bangladesh must raise the minimum wage and install wage reviews in the country.[38] However, Persson said nothing about his own personal responsibility in the matter, or that workers' wages are also tied to H&M's payment to its manufacturers.

In brand communication, one talks about USP and ESP – Unique Selling Proposition and Emotional Selling Proposition. That is to say, the shape an ad takes in order to sell a product. One can play on a product's uniqueness or the emotions surrounding it.[39] In the last few years, a new abbreviation has emerged: ETSP – Ethical Selling Proposition: ads whose focus is on ethical values.[40]

This might indicate that Portas and Shepherdson are indeed right in claiming that shopping's 'feel-good effect' is dwindling. The question is whether this new set of ethics is a widespread reaction that will come to change the market and save the world. The alternative, of course, is that it is simply a pretext to shop as before, only with a better conscience.

For their part, the pioneers associated with Arnold Circus in London started with some empty retail spaces in an old neighbourhood. This was the city's worst slum in the 1800s, with its high criminality and child mortality rates, and its widespread prostitution on street corners. Jack the Ripper prowled the area in his day. However, at the start of the 1900s people decided to do something about the misery. Decent living accommodation was built for the poor: Victorian, solid, red-brick buildings. And around the small park, today called Arnold Circus, the buildings were built in a circle so that the green area with its central pavilion would be the area's natural hub.

By the mid-2000s, however, the neighbourhood was no longer attractive. The park was a wilderness no one wanted to use, and the corner shop was gone. Right in the city, Arnold Circus was becoming a ghost town. Then there came a gang of designers, artists and creative folk who saw beauty in the weeds. They wanted to give the neighbourhood with the park at its heart new life. At the centre of the new initiative was, among other things, Leila's Shop, a café and boutique with fruit and vegetables and a selection of high-quality food wares. Food is served on wooden boards and the washing up is done by hand. Coffee-to-go does not exist. If you want a sip, you sit down and enjoy it in a real cup. While you sip, you can watch street life or see the food prepared on a kitchen island in the middle of the room. Leila's is not about consumption. It is about enjoying oneself and appreciating the moment. Objects conceptualize the new simplicity. Bicycles parked outside are often old and used, with a functional crate strapped to the luggage rack. Chairs, tables and cutlery, as well as the café's entire inventory, are simple, solid and sustainable. In the shop vegetables are displayed like artworks in old enamelled bowls and on crates. The people who come here seem to think: life isn't about consumption, it is about attentiveness, quality and enjoyment. Natural but cool hair; simple but trendy clothes; recycling down to the very last detail.

Interior stylist and author Emily Chalmers works near Leila's and thinks that this basics-based approach enables people to enjoy themselves. When consumption in society is in the midst of overflowing, like it is now, it is authenticity that makes them stop and think. 'It is extremely refreshing that they don't have takeaway coffee at Leila's', she says. 'When you drink coffee there, you have the little glass, the teaspoon, the sugar in the coffee and a nice pot. It is about appreciating the small things, not the pretentiousness that has become common in so many other places. Sometimes there isn't room at Leila's either, you have to wait on a spot and that's just the way it is. You can't get everything you want'.[41]

BioCouture designer Suzanne Lee also sees signs of a new and conscious spring. There is a greater focus on recycling and less on the consumption of fashion. However, it is to a certain extent a class phenomenon. The movement is located in the educated, urbane British middle class – not in the populace at large. It is often those with fewer resources that still stuff their bags full of bargain clothes at Primark.

Perhaps notching down is simply a sign that you are a socially conscious aesthete with a brain – a way to distinguish yourself by turning your back on fashion's stereotypes. Perhaps it is merely a reaction to the wild buying frenzy that dulled down before the financial crisis woke everybody up. Perhaps people must just find new and cheaper ways to get things they want, because there is simply less money to throw around.

However, it is also trendy. It is hip to be aware. A head on top of a beautiful body is in style. Fashion is the found and unique item that someone else has used before. That means that the transformation that Mary Portas and Jane Shepherdson see coming – from fast to ethical – has an uncertain prognosis. That means that perhaps a great revolution is not under way and that we are not witnessing the emergence of a lasting and sustainable restructuring of consumption patterns. Perhaps people are just once again caught up by what is fashionable. For a brief moment, ethical consumers are the elite who are allowed to show the way. If so, a new fashion and a new group will take over after that. The simple life will be replaced by something fresh, and once-sustainable shopping habits will be lost. This ethical element in fashion reveals itself as a shallow form of goodwill. That means that Kate Middleton can be seen to be recycling by the press because she wears the same dress to more than one public appearance. Wearing a dress twice has nothing to do with environmentally friendly recycling. Green words are simply used because they are fashionable. Like the story about the Japanese who embraced the Christmas decoration wave and made ornaments with Santa Claus rather unfortunately nailed to the cross. They meant well, but it was a superficial gesture. It was not completely authentic.

Fast-fashion chains launch charitable campaigns where they sell apparel to collect money for the fight against AIDS and breast cancer, to support SOS Children's Villages and so forth. The fashion industry arranges celebrity shows in support of weaker groups. All that is wonderful – but it also has an air of hypocrisy. You do not make any actual progress, other than making shoppers feel a bit better and giving away some money. We attribute a positive effect to things without the negative effect actually being absent.

Why the Brain is Not Green

We are not smart. If we know something to be true, after all, we ought to be able to use that knowledge and act accordingly. If we receive the message that our very future depends on decreasing consumption, we ought not to increase it, and certainly not on dress items. What is it that prevents people from thinking green?

A group at Columbia University decided to look for the answer. Its Center for Research on Environmental Decisions (CRED) consists of economists, psychologists and anthropologists. Together they explore how people individually and in groups make decisions with regard to questions of climate change. New environmentally friendly technologies and government initiatives aren't enough to solve the issues introduced by global warming. Since these problems are created by human behavioural patterns, they must be solved by changing that behaviour. Therefore, CRED focuses on how people act and what is required for those actions to change. As it turns out, we have some basic mental predispositions that do not incline towards forests of gold and green. We view loss more negatively than gain. We don't like to wait for good things to come our way, but want immediate results. If we have a choice between receiving $100 today or $200 in two years, we opt to pocket the $100 bill. People also have a hard time juggling too many fears at once. When a new anxiety enters the scene, old ones are discarded. Therefore, it is difficult to worry about global warming in the face of a major financial crisis. In this case, concern for the environment gives way. And to patch up our conscience and conceal our Judas streak, we might decide to vote Green in the next election or to buy a few environmentally friendly products that might provide some benefit.

So are we even capable of tackling today's global issues? Long-term thinking is difficult for us. We are shaped to confront immediate dangers, such as predator attacks. A doomsday prophecy that might come to pass 90 years from now has a more difficult time eliciting a response – even if the ultimatum exists today. The human brain doesn't seem wired to deal with these types of scenarios.

However, there are certain devices that do encourage us to react more promptly. We are willing to sacrifice more if we have a sense of group belonging. Concrete information also motivates us to act. On the other hand, we are hampered by critique and unanswered questions. Ultimately, it is our fear of and experience with danger that most effectively sparks a reaction.[42] 'Increasing personal evidence of global warming and its potentially devastating consequences can be counted on to be an extremely effective teacher and motivator', Professor Elke Weber of CRED observes. 'Unfortunately, such lessons may arrive too late for corrective action.'[43]

In the film *The Man in the White Suit*, Sidney Stratton (Alec Guinness) dreams of inventing a material that never rips or stains – a material that allows people to wear one single garment their entire lives with no washing, repairing, discarding or repurchasing required. The thought is so amazing that the inventor devotes every hour of the day to his experiments. Inside the laboratory at the textile factory where he works, he has built an odd construction of reagent tubes and flasks that are nothing like what the others have. One day the CEO realizes what Stratton is actually doing. Just like Stratton, the dream of the everlasting intoxicates and obsesses him. He orders the laboratory to be cleared of all other activity. Stratton will receive free rein and all the resources he needs to develop his new material. And one day the miraculous occurs. The experiment is a success. Stratton has invented something that will forever replace all other textiles. They are able to spin a thread, they weave a piece of cloth and, with the help of some welding equipment, they cut and sew the first – and last – suit human beings will ever need. It is the white suit. Now all that remains is the final agreement with the factory – and the world is saved.

However, the industry leaders have changed their minds. What will happen to production if the need for new clothes is a thing of the past? How are they supposed to earn money? What will happen to stock exchanges around the world? No, a permanent material will have a catastrophic effect on the world's economy. And beyond the office doors the workers have also dug in their heels. They think that Stratton's invention will leave them unemployed and cost them power and rights. Sidney Stratton must be stopped; there is no other way. Propelled by greed and fear of the unknown, the hunt for the man in the white suit is on. Together the bosses, the union men and the workers pursue Stratton through the streets like a wild animal. Finally, he is trapped in a corner and his pursuers are ready to attack. But then, of all things, they start laughing – it sounds almost hearty – as if in profound relief. Sidney Stratton looks around him in confusion. He doesn't understand. Not before people start grabbing at his suit. Then he realizes they are holding bits of cloth in their hands. The incredible everlasting material that could not be stained or torn has begun to disintegrate. The chemical compound turns out to be unstable. The dream of the infinite was just that – a dream.[44]

Released in 1951, the film was billed as a comedy. Today it is a metaphor for capitalism's widespread authority and people's fear of the new and unknown. In the years since its release, *The Man in the White Suit* has become a cult film in academic fashion circles. It is admirably clear-sighted, considering it was made at a time when moderation was still the goal. Some people think we ought to return to the consumption levels they had back then, that it would be enough to sink consumption to what was normal in the 1960s. That doesn't necessarily mean that we should return to 1960s technology and adopt an outdated lifestyle, however. Indeed, some believe it is by virtue of today's technology that we can return to feasible consumption levels.

In the documentary *The Light Bulb Conspiracy*, the Internet is represented as the light at the tunnel's end. The first-generation iPods were equipped with a battery that lasted only eighteen months. When the batteries gave out, people were forced to buy a new iPod. This was so alarming that it prompted a massive on-line campaign. The campaign led to a class action lawsuit against Apple in 2003, filed by consumers themselves. The suit ended in a settlement. Apple had to redesign the iPod with interchangeable batteries, and battery life was increased to two years.[45] The Internet made it possible for individual consumers to wield power in the marketplace. It was the tool required to mobilize enough people to achieve a collective reaction. Some people think that such collectivism can be the solution.[46]

In this kind of society, people's focus will shift from 'me' to 'us'. Then the power of the collective will increase and consumers and workers can wield real power against producers and other capitalistic forces. Then it is no longer a case of a mouse peeing in the ocean. Then it is actually possible to do something about collective consumption, manufacturing relationships and the capitalistic system. Then people can perform Nemo's trick: swim in the same direction so that the ship follows the fish and not the reverse.

However, collectivism won't occur simply on the basis of new and widespread technology. Every single person must still choose to value 'us' in order for a collective spirit to emerge. Something must force people to open their eyes and choose a different way of thinking and, along with that, a different social system. Once again it all boils down to the individual.

There is nothing wrong with looking good. To be beautiful in your own eyes, to dress yourself up for others, to visually create and communicate. These things are natural and have been so for thousands of years. The negative here is the imbalance that has entered the system. Consumption of decoration and dress items is too high – the focus on attractive appearance and having new things too strong. We are more concerned with impressing each other than caring for each other. The catalyst that has boosted and continues to boost this development is capitalism. It is the unidirectional economic approach to eternal growth and profit that has spun the act of dressing out of all proportion. The desire for economic gain ensures that the fashion industry produces too high a quantity at too low a quality, thereby trampling on people in the process. In addition, the industry seduces people into wanting and buying more than they need. And people open themselves up to temptation. As a result, the notion of 'looking good' is about more than beauty. We can't keep doubling our consumption of dress items every twenty years. As it stands today, our consumption levels aren't sustainable. Eventually, something must give. The question is whether or not permanent damage will have occurred when consumption is finally reduced.

In *The Matrix*, the evil Agent Smith acts as the machines' executioner. He has been sent to crush the rebel, Neo, and to end forever humanity's struggle for freedom. Only then can the machines' world domination continue as before. In one of the scenes Agent Smith reveals something about the history of the Matrix, the data program that plants experiences of a normal life inside people's heads. The agent says that the first version of the program was a beautiful one. It allowed people to experience a perfect world where no one suffered and all were happy. The program was a catastrophe. People refused to accept it. They kept trying to wake up – as if it were all a dream. People were not built for perpetual happiness and well-being. There must be something negative, destructive and unjust in order for the human brain to accept the scenario.

It is entirely possible that a dream of everyone doing right and dancing together in the meadow dressed in solid, conscientious and environmentally friendly garments – of which they will not have too many – is like the first version of the Matrix. Giving up advantage is something people do only if they absolutely must. And when they realize this is necessary, it might already be too late. Irreparable harm might already have occurred. In this case, it will be the consequences that wake people up. However, that doesn't mean that humanity stops striving towards sacred objectives. The most common story of all is the fight between good and evil – where good triumphs at last.

References

Introduction

1 See, for example, SOURCE Intelligence, www.ethicalfashionforum. com.

2 Sandy Black, *The Sustainable Fashion Handbook* (London, 2012), p. 15.

ONE Human Beings

1 'Urbane stammer', *D2* (21 November 2008)

2 *The Beales of Grey Gardens*, dir. Albert Maysles and David Maysles (2006).

3 *Grey Gardens*, dir. Michael Sucsy (2009).

4 'Shakira and Pink Wear Same Dress to VMAs: Who Wore it Better?', www.huffingtonpost.com, 14 November 2009.

5 ' – Noen vil få sparken for dette', www.kjendis.no, 19 May 2011.

6 *Single White Female*, dir. Barbet Schroeder (1992).

7 'Provoserende plagg', *D2* (26 November 2010), pp. 13 and 19.

8 Joanne Turney, 'As Seen on CCTV – Anti-social Knitting and the Horror of the "Hoodie"' (Bath Spa University, 2009).

9 Joanne Turney, interview with the author, January 2010.

10 Ibid.

11 Anne-Louise Sommer et al., eds, *FLUX: Research at the Danish Design School* (Copenhagen, 2009), p. 100.

12 Interview with Li Edelkoort in 'Designens DNA', *Personae*, I/1 (2008), p. 14.

13 Maria Mackinney-Valentin, *On the Nature of Trends: A Study of Trend Mechanisms in Contemporary Fashion* (Copenhagen, 2010).

14 'Roten til alt flott', interview with the author, *Personae*, II/2 (2009), p. 12.

15 'Forsteder i flammer', www.morgenbladet.no, 4 November 2005.

16 Mari Grinde Arntzen, 'Snurpete mote', *A-magasinet* (9 June 2006), p. 47.

17 'Roten til alt flott', p. 15.

18 Ibid.

19 Ibid.

20 Ibid.

21 Lars Svendsen, *Fashion: A Philosophy* (London, 2006), p. 28.

22 Sommer et al., eds, *FLUX*, pp. 104–5.

23 'Roten til alt flott', p. 14.

24 Dita Von Teese, *Burlesque and the Art of the Teese* (New York, 2006), p. xxi.

25 Mari Grinde Arntzen, 'Hetteskrekk', *A-magasinet* (11 May 2007), p. 46.

26 Svendsen, *Fashion*.

27 Editorial, *Personae*, I/1 (2008), p. 3.

28 Tamsin Blanchard, 'Rebel de jour', www.guardian.co.uk, 15 August 2004.

29 Lucy Cavendish, 'The Not So Mad Hatter', www.telegraph.co.uk, 15 January 2006.

30 Sophie Woodward, *Why Woman Wear What They Wear* (Oxford, 2007), pp. 1–2.

31 Ibid., pp. 85–8.

32 Ibid., p. 2.

33 Ibid., p. 83.

34 Anne Boultwood and Robert Jerrard, 'Ambivalence, and its Relation to Fashion and the Body', *Fashion Theory*, IV/3 (2000), p. 310.

35 Woodward, *Why Women Wear What They Wear*, pp. 96–7.

TWO The Democracy

1 Mari Grinde Arntzen, 'Raske skift', *A-magasinet* (13 April 2007), p. 46.
2 Ibid., pp. 47–8.
3 See *Dagens Handel*, www.dagenshandel.se, 8 February 2006.
4 See Gina Tricot, www.ginatricot.com.
5 'Faktaark om forbruk', FIVH, www.framtiden.no (September 2009).
6 'Neppe en lønn å leve av', FIVH, www.framtiden.no (March 2009).
7 Sandy Black, *The Sustainable Fashion Handbook* (London, 2012), p. 9.
8 Worldwatch Institute, www.worldwatch.org.
9 See H&M, www.hm.com.
10 Lars Svendsen, *Fashion: A Philosophy* (London, 2006).
11 Bonnie English, *A Cultural History of Fashion in the 20th Century: From the Catwalk to the Sidewalk* (Oxford, 2007), pp. 8–10.
12 Ibid., p. 31.
13 Ibid., p. 34.
14 Ibid., p. 42.
15 Ibid., p. 82.
16 *British Style Genius* (TV series, BBC Two, 2008).
17 See Style.com, www.style.com.
18 'An Interview with Alber Elbaz', www.video.nytimes.com, 9 November 2010.
19 *Vogue* (UK, November 2009), p. 160.

THREE Dictatorship

1 *The September Issue*, dir. R. J. Cutler (2009).
2 Ibid.
3 Elsa Beskow, *The Flowers' Festival* (Edinburgh, 1999).
4 Ibid.
5 'Den demokratiske mode?', seminar at the Royal Danish Academy of Fine Arts, School of Design, 5 October 2009.
6 Johnny Davis, 'Style Journal *Fantastic Man*: It's a Man Thing', *The Times* (17 October 2009).

7 Mari Grinde Arntzen andd Kristoffer Rønneberg, 'I kø for å føle seg rike', *A-magasinet* (17 November 2006), p. 46.

8 Ibid., p. 49.

9 Dana Thomas, *Deluxe: How Luxury Lost its Lustre* (London, 2007), p. 324.

10 Anne Boultwood and Robert Jerrard, 'Ambivalence, and its Relation to Fashion and the Body', *Fashion Theory*, IV/3 (2000), p. 301.

11 Kim K. P. Johnson and Sharron J. Lennon, *Appearance and Power* (Oxford, 1999), p. 59.

12 Ibid., p. 63.

13 Ibid., p. 61.

14 Ibid., p. 62.

15 '– Kvinner må være pene for å få jobb', www.dagbladet.no, 9 September 2008.

16 S. K. Johnson et al., 'Physical Attractiveness Biases in Ratings of Employment Suitability: Tracking Down the "Beauty is Beastly" Effect', *Journal of Social Psychology* (May–June 2010).

17 'Pyntedukker underveis', www.aftenposten.no, 4 May 2011.

18 *Shallow Hal*, dir. Bobby and Peter Farrelly (2001).

19 TV 2 Nyhetene, www.tv2nyhetene.no.

20 www.dagbladet.no, 28 August 2009.

21 'Pent ansikt sanker stemmer', www.forsking.no, 3 November 2008.

22 Jane Pavitt, *Fear and Fashion in the Cold War* (London, 2008).

23 Eugenia Paulicelli, *Fashion under Fascism: Beyond the Black Shirt* (Oxford, 2004), p. 21.

24 Lars Svendsen, *Fashion: A Philosophy* (London, 2006), p. 37.

25 Mari Grinde Arntzen, 'Rustfri Kriger', *Personae*, III/4 (2001), p. 36.

26 'Torstein Veblen. Mote og klassifisering', *Personae*, I (2009), p. 134.

27 Johnson and Lennon, *Appearance and Power*, pp. 173–92.

FOUR The Brain

1 Anne Boultwood and Robert Jerrard, 'Ambivalence, and its Relation to Fashion and the Body', *Fashion Theory*, IV/3 (2000), p. 301.

2 Ibid., p. 306.

3   Mari Grinde Arntzen, 'Størrelsen teller', *A-magasinet*
    (9 November 2007), p. 49.

4   Bjørn Schiermer, 'Fashion Victims: On the Individualizing
    and De-individualizing Powers of Fashion', *Fashion Theory*,
    XIV/1 (March 2010), p. 97.

5   Lucy Cavendish, 'The Not So Mad Hatter',
    www.telegraph.co.uk, 15 January 2006.

6   Tamsin Blanchard, 'Rebel de jour', www.guardian.co.uk,
    15 August 2004.

7   Edward Helmore, 'Final Blow', *Vanity Fair* (September 2007),
    p. 230.

8   'Pene barn får mer omsorg', www.forskning.no, 21 April 2005.

9   'Du digger pene mennesker', www.forskning.no, 15 August
    2008.

10 'Pent ansikt sanker stemmer', www.forskning.no, 3 November
    2008.

11 'Forveksler skjønnhet og sannhet', www.forskning.no,
    8 November 2008.

12 'Tunisias Lady Macbeth', *Klassekampen* (12 March 2011),
    pp. 16–19.

13 'Skjønnhet og helse – det ytre og indre', *SIFO*, report nr.
    1-2011, p. 8, available at www.sifo.no.

14 Ibid.

15 'Etterlyser en lesbepatrulje', *Klassekampen* (12 March 2001),
    p. 40.

16 *VG*, www.vg.no, 8 March 2010.

17 Fay Weldon, *The Life and Loves of a She-Devil* (London, 1983).

18 *She-Devil* (1989), www.imdb.com.

19 The Literature, Arts, and Medicine Database,
    http://litmed.med.nyu.edu.

20 Roger Scruton, *Why Beauty Matters* (TV documentary, BBC
    Two, 2009).

21 Ibid.

22 Peter Waits, 'The Cult of Beauty: The Peacock Artists who
    Ruffled Feathers', www.independent.co.uk, 20 March 2011.

23 Edward Helmore, 'Final Blow', *Vanity Fair* (September 2007),
    p. 238.

24 Boultwood and Jerrard, 'Ambivalence, and its Relation to
    Fashion and the Body', p. 314.

25 Lionel Bailly, *Lacan: A Beginner's Guide* (Oxford, 2009), p. 29.

26 Joanne Turney, interview with the author, January 2010.
27 Helmore, 'Final Blow', p. 236.

FIVE The Future

1 Stuart Jeffries, 'The Saturday Interview: Vivienne Westwood', www.guardian.co.uk, 3 December 2011.
2 Ibid.
3 See Fashion Revolution, www.fashionrevolutionusa.org.
4 Sandy Black, *The Sustainable Fashion Handbook* (London, 2012), p. 9.
5 'Neppe en lønn å leve av', FIVH, www.framtiden.no (2009).
6 Ibid.
7 'Betaler prisen', *Magasinet Dagbladet* (31 May 2014), p. 22.
8 Initiativ for Etisk Handel, www.etiskhandel.no.
9 'Skitne klær', FORUM (December 2008), at naturvernforbundet .no, pp. 37–8.
10 Ibid., p. 35.
11 'Bruker tre år av livet på shopping', www.minmote.no, 13 April 2010.
12 Kirsi Maria Laitala, Ingun Grimstad Klepp and Casper Boks, 'Changing Laundry Habits in Norway', *International Journal of Consumer Studies*, XXXVI/2 (2012), www.sifo.no.
13 See WRAP (Waste and Resources Action Programme), www.wrap.org.uk.
14 Tansy E. Hoskins, 'The Trouble With Second-hand Clothes', www.businessoffashion.com, 10 November 2013.
15 *The Light Bulb Conspiracy*, dir. Cosima Dannoritzer (2010).
16 *Familia*, online magazine of the Norwegian Ministry of Children, Equality and Social Inclusion, www.regjeringen.no (February 2007).
17 See 350.org, www.350.org.
18 Fiona Harvey, 'World Headed for Irreversible Climate Change in Five Years, IEA Warns', www.guardian.co.uk, 9 November 2011.
19 Fiona Harvey, 'Worst Ever Carbon Emissions Leave Climate on the Brink', www.guardian.co.uk, 29 May 2011.
20 'Vent deg våtere vintre', www.aftenposten.no, 18 November 2011.
21 'IPCC Press Release', www.ipcc.ch, 31 March 2014.

22 Suzanne Goldenberg, 'Climate Change a Threat to Security, Food and Humankind – IPCC Report', www.guardian.co.uk, 31 March 2014.

23 'Faktaark om forbruk', FIVH, www.framtiden.no (March 2011).

24 James Lovelock, 'Enjoy Life While You Can', www.guardian.co.uk, 1 March 2008.

25 Jeffries, 'The Saturday Interview: Vivienne Westwood'.

26 *The Light Bulb Conspiracy*, dir. Dannoritzer.

27 Tejinder Singh, 'The Dalai Lama Blames "Greed" for Financial Crisis', *New Europe*, www.neurope.eu, 8 December 2008.

28 'Förenkla ditt liv – få tid att leva', slogan of the Swedish interior design chain Granit.

29 Simon Moss, 'Theory of Planned Behaviour', *Psychlopedia*, www.psych-it.com.au, 18 October 2008.

30 Daniel Miller, *A Theory of Shopping* (Ithaca, NY, 1998), p. 138.

31 Colin Beavan, 'The Place of Desire', www.noimpactman. typepad.com, 18 April 2011.

32 Mari Grinde Arntzen, 'Designspiren', D2 (13 May 2011), p. 63.

33 Ibid.

34 Ibid.

35 *British Style Genius* (TV series, BBC Two, 2008).

36 'Mary Portas: From Fast Fashion to a More Considered Consumerism', www.fashion.telegraph.co.uk, 31 October 2010.

37 *British Style Genius* (BBC Two).

38 'H&M ber om mer lønn til arbeidere', *Klassekampen* (8 September 2012), p. 30.

39 Bo Bergström, *Essentials of Visual Communication* (London, 2008), pp. 64–6.

40 Ibid., p. 66.

41 Mari Grinde Arntzen, 'Det langsomme liv i London', *Dagbladet Søndag* (23 August 2009), p. 41.

42 Jon Gernter, 'Why Isn't the Brain Green?', *New York Times Magazine*, www.nytimes.com, 16 April 2009.

43 Ibid.

44 *The Man in The White Suit*, dir. Alexander Mackendrick (1951).

45 *The Light Bulb Conspiracy*, dir. Dannoritzer.

46 Bradley Quinn, *Design Futures* (London, 2011), p. 215.